A Brief History of the English Language and Literature, Vol. 2 (of 2)

by

John Miller Dow Meiklejohn

The Echo Library 2008

Published by

The Echo Library

Echo Library
131 High St.
Teddington
Middlesex TW11 8HH

www.echo-library.com

Please report serious faults in the text to complaints@echo-library.com

ISBN 978-1-40687-461-7

PREFACE.

This book provides sufficient matter for the four years of study required, in England, of a pupil-teacher, and also for the first year at his training college. An experienced master will easily be able to guide his pupils in the selection of the proper parts for each year. The ten pages on the Grammar of Verse ought to be reserved for the fifth year of study.

It is hoped that the book will also be useful in Colleges, Ladies' Seminaries, High Schools, Academies, Preparatory and Normal Schools, to candidates for teachers' examinations and Civil Service examinations, and to all who wish for any reason to review the leading facts of the English Language and Literature.

Only the most salient features of the language have been described, and minor details have been left for the teacher to fill in. The utmost clearness and simplicity have been the aim of the writer, and he has been obliged to sacrifice many interesting details to this aim.

The study of English Grammar is becoming every day more and more historical— and necessarily so. There are scores of inflections, usages, constructions, idioms, which cannot be truly or adequately explained without a reference to the past states of the language— to the time when it was a synthetic or inflected language, like German or Latin.

The Syntax of the language has been set forth in the form of RULES. This was thought to be better for young learners who require firm and clear dogmatic statements of fact and duty. But the skilful teacher will slowly work up to these rules by the interesting process of induction, and will— when it is possible— induce his pupil to draw the general conclusions from the data given, and thus to make rules for himself. Another convenience that will be found by both teacher and pupil in this form of rules will be that they can be compared with the rules of, or general statements about, a foreign language— such as Latin, French, or German.

It is earnestly hoped that the slight sketches of the History of our Language and of its Literature may not only enable the young student to pass his examinations with success, but may also throw him into the attitude of mind of Oliver Twist, and induce him to "ask for more."

The Index will be found useful in preparing the parts of each subject; as all the separate paragraphs about the same subject will be found there grouped together.

J. M. D. M.

4

CONTENTS.

PART III.

The English Language, and the Family to which it belongs
The Periods of English
History of the Vocabulary
History of the Grammar
Specimens of English of Different Periods
Modern English
Landmarks in the History of the English Language

PART IV.

History of English Literature
Tables of English Literature
Index

PART III.

THE HISTORY OF THE ENGLISH LANGUAGE

INTRODUCTION.

1. Tongue, Speech, Language.— We speak of the "English tongue" or of the "French language"; and we say of two nations that they "do not understand each other's speech." The existence of these three words— speech, tongue, language— proves to us that a language is something spoken,— that it is a number of sounds; and that the writing or printing of it upon paper is a quite secondary matter. Language, rightly considered, then, is an organised set of sounds. These sounds convey a meaning from the mind of the speaker to the mind of the hearer, and thus serve to connect man with man.

2. Written Language.— It took many hundreds of years— perhaps thousands— before human beings were able to invent a mode of writing upon paper— that is, of representing sounds by signs. These signs are called letters; and the whole set of them goes by the name of the Alphabet— from the two first letters of the Greek alphabet, which are called alpha, beta. There are languages that have never been put upon paper at all, such as many of the African languages, many in the South Sea Islands, and other parts of the globe. But in all cases, every language that we know anything about— English, Latin, French, German— existed for hundreds of years before any one thought of writing it down on paper.

3. A Language Grows.— A language is an organism or organic existence. Now every organism lives; and, if it lives, it grows; and, if it grows, it also dies. Our language grows; it is growing still; and it has been growing for many hundreds of years. As it grows it loses something, and it gains something else; it alters its appearance; changes take place in this part of it and in that part,— until at length its appearance in age is something almost entirely different from what it was in its early youth. If we had the photograph of a man of forty, and the photograph of the same person when he was a child of one, we should find, on comparing them, that it was almost impossible to point to the smallest trace of likeness in the features of the two photographs. And yet the two pictures represent the same person. And so it is with the English language. The oldest English, which is usually called Anglo-Saxon, is as different from our modern English as if they were two distinct languages; and yet they are not two languages, but really and fundamentally one and the same. Modern English differs from the oldest English as a giant oak does from a small oak sapling, or a broad stalwart man of forty does from a feeble infant of a few months old.

4. The English Language.— The English language is the speech spoken by the Anglo-Saxon race in England, in most parts of Scotland, in the larger part of Ireland, in the United States, in Canada, in Australia and New Zealand, in South Africa, and in many other parts of the world. In the middle of the fifth century it was spoken by a few thousand men who had lately landed in England from the Continent: it is now spoken by more than one hundred millions of people. In

the course of the next sixty years, it will probably be the speech of two hundred millions.

5. English on the Continent.— In the middle of the fifth century it was spoken in the north-west corner of Europe— between the mouths of the Rhine, the Weser, and the Elbe; and in Schleswig there is a small district which is called Angeln to this day. But it was not then called English; it was more probably called Teutish, or Teutsch, or Deutsch— all words connected with a generic word which covers many families and languages— Teutonic. It was a rough guttural speech of one or two thousand words; and it was brought over to this country by the Jutes, Angles, and Saxons in the year 449. These men left their home on the Continent to find here farms to till and houses to live in; and they drove the inhabitants of the island— the Britons— ever farther and farther west, until they at length left them in peace in the more mountainous parts of the island— in the southern and western corners, in Cornwall and in Wales.

6. The British Language.— What language did the Teutonic conquerors, who wrested the lands from the poor Britons, find spoken in this island when they first set foot on it? Not a Teutonic speech at all. They found a language not one word of which they could understand. The island itself was then called Britain; and the tongue spoken in it belonged to the Keltic group of languages. Languages belonging to the Keltic group are still spoken in Wales, in Brittany (in France), in the Highlands of Scotland, in the west of Ireland, and in the Isle of Man. A few words— very few— from the speech of the Britons, have come into our own English language; and what these are we shall see by-and-by.

7. The Family to which English belongs.— Our English tongue belongs to the Aryan or Indo-European Family of languages. That is to say, the main part or substance of it can be traced back to the race which inhabited the high table-lands that lie to the back of the western end of the great range of the Himalaya, or "Abode of Snow." This Aryan race grew and increased, and spread to the south and west; and from it have sprung languages which are now spoken in India, in Persia, in Greece and Italy, in France and Germany, in Scandinavia, and in Russia. From this Aryan family we are sprung; out of the oldest Aryan speech our own language has grown.

8. The Group to which English belongs.— The Indo-European family of languages consists of several groups. One of these is called the Teutonic Group, because it is spoken by the Teuts (or the Teutonic race), who are found in Germany, in England and Scotland, in Holland, in parts of Belgium, in Denmark, in Norway and Sweden, in Iceland, and the Faroe Islands. The Teutonic group consists of three branches— High German, Low German, and Scandinavian. High German is the name given to the kind of German spoken in Upper Germany— that is, in the table-land which lies south of the river Main, and which rises gradually till it runs into the Alps. New High German is the German of books— the literary language— the German that is taught and learned in schools. Low German is the name given to the German dialects spoken in the lowlands— in the German part of the Great Plain of Europe, and round the mouths of those German rivers that flow into the Baltic and the

North Sea. Scandinavian is the name given to the languages spoken in Denmark and in the great Scandinavian Peninsula. Of these three languages, Danish and Norwegian are practically the same— their literary or book-language is one; while Swedish is very different. Icelandic is the oldest and purest form of Scandinavian. The following is a table of the

GROUP OF TEUTONIC LANGUAGES.

[The table was originally printed in full family-tree form, using the layout below. The full text is here given separately.]

```
              T.
        ——|——
        |       |       |
       LG      HG      Sc
    ——|——   |    ——|——
    |  |  | |  | | |  | | | |
   Du Fl Fr E  O M N  I Dk Fe Sv
                (Nk) (Sw)
```

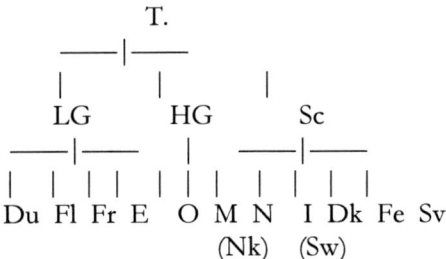

TEUTONIC.
LOW GERMAN.
Dutch.
Flemish.
Frisian.
English.
HIGH GERMAN.
Old.
Middle.
New.
SCANDINAVIAN.
Icelandic
Dansk
(or Norsk).
Ferroic.
Svensk
(Swedish).

It will be observed, on looking at the above table, that High German is subdivided according to time, but that the other groups are subdivided according to space.

9. English a Low-German Speech.— Our English tongue is the lowest of all Low-German dialects. Low German is the German spoken in the lowlands of Germany. As we descend the rivers, we come to the lowest level of all— the level of the sea. Our English speech, once a mere dialect, came down to that, crossed the German Ocean, and settled in Britain, to which it gave in time the name of Angla-land or England. The Low German spoken in the Netherlands is

called Dutch; the Low German spoken in Friesland— a prosperous province of Holland— is called Frisian; and the Low German spoken in Great Britain is called English. These three languages are extremely like one another; but the Continental language that is likest the English is the Dutch or Hollandish dialect called Frisian. We even possess a couplet, every word of which is both English and Frisian. It runs thus—

Good butter and good cheese
Is good English and good Fries.

10. Dutch and Welsh— a Contrast.— When the Teuton conquerors came to this country, they called the Britons foreigners, just as the Greeks called all other peoples besides themselves barbarians. By this they did not at first mean that they were uncivilised, but only that they were not Greeks. Now, the Teutonic or Saxon or English name for foreigners was Wealhas, a word afterwards contracted into Welsh. To this day the modern Teuts or Teutons (or Germans, as we call them) call all Frenchmen and Italians Welshmen; and, when a German, peasant crosses the border into France, he says: "I am going into Welshland."

11. The Spread of English over Britain.— The Jutes, who came from Juteland or Jylland— now called Jutland— settled in Kent and in the Isle of Wight. The Saxons settled in the south and western parts of England, and gave their names to those kingdoms— now counties— whose names came to end in sex. There was the kingdom of the East Saxons, or Essex; the kingdom of the West Saxons, or Wessex; the kingdom of the Middle Saxons, or Middlesex; and the kingdom of the South Saxons, or Sussex. The Angles settled chiefly on the east coast. The kingdom of East Anglia was divided into the regions of the North Folk and the South Folk, words which are still perpetuated in the names Norfolk and Suffolk. These three sets of Teutons all spoke different dialects of the same Teutonic speech; and these dialects, with their differences, peculiarities, and odd habits, took root in English soil, and lived an independent life, apart from each other, uninfluenced by each other, for several hundreds of years. But, in the slow course of time, they joined together to make up our beautiful English language— a language which, however, still bears in itself the traces of dialectic forms, and is in no respect of one kind or of one fibre all through.

CHAPTER I.

THE PERIODS OF ENGLISH.

1. Dead and Living Languages.— A language is said to be dead when it is no longer spoken. Such a language we know only in books. Thus, Latin is a dead language, because no nation anywhere now speaks it. A dead language can undergo no change; it remains, and must remain, as we find it written in books. But a living language is always changing, just like a tree or the human body. The human body has its periods or stages. There is the period of infancy, the period of boyhood, the period of manhood, and the period of old age. In the same way, a language has its periods.

2. No Sudden Changes— a Caution.— We divide the English language into periods, and then mark, with some approach to accuracy, certain distinct changes in the habits of our language, in the inflexions of its words, in the kind of words it preferred, or in the way it liked to put its words together. But we must be carefully on our guard against fancying that, at any given time or in any given year, the English people threw aside one set of habits as regards language, and adopted another set. It is not so, nor can it be so. The changes in language are as gentle, gradual, and imperceptible as the changes in the growth of a tree or in the skin of the human body. We renew our skin slowly and gradually; but we are never conscious of the process, nor can we say at any given time that we have got a completely new skin.

3. The Periods of English.— Bearing this caution in mind, we can go on to look at the chief periods in our English language. These are five in number; and they are as follows:—

I. Ancient English or Anglo-Saxon,	449-1100
II. Early English,	1100-1250
III. Middle English,	1250-1485
IV. Tudor English,	1485-1603
V. Modern English,	1603-1900

These periods merge very slowly, or are shaded off, so to speak, into each other in the most gradual way. If we take the English of 1250 and compare it with that of 900, we shall find a great difference; but if we compare it with the English of 1100 the difference is not so marked. The difference between the English of the nineteenth and the English of the fourteenth century is very great, but the difference between the English of the fourteenth and that of the thirteenth century is very small.

4. Ancient English or Anglo-Saxon, 450-1100.— This form of English differed from modern English in having a much larger number of inflexions. The noun had five cases, and there were several declensions, just as in Latin; adjectives were declined, and had three genders; some pronouns had a dual as well as a plural number; and the verb had a much larger number of inflexions

than it has now. The vocabulary of the language contained very few foreign elements. The poetry of the language employed head-rhyme or alliteration, and not end-rhyme, as we do now. The works of the poet Caedmon and the great prose-writer King Alfred belong to this Anglo-Saxon period.

5. Early English, 1100-1250.— The coming of the Normans in 1066 made many changes in the land, many changes in the Church and in the State, and it also introduced many changes into the language. The inflexions of our speech began to drop off, because they were used less and less; and though we never adopted new inflexions from French or from any other language, new French words began to creep in. In some parts of the country English had ceased to be written in books; the language existed as a spoken language only; and hence accuracy in the use of words and the inflexions of words could not be ensured. Two notable books— written, not printed, for there was no printing in this island till the year 1474— belong to this period. These are the Ormulum, by Orm or Ormin, and the Brut, by a monk called Layamon or Laweman. The latter tells the story of Brutus, who was believed to have been the son of Æneas of Troy; to have escaped after the downfall of that city; to have sailed through the Mediterranean, ever farther and farther to the west; to have landed in Britain, settled here, and given the country its name.

6. Middle English, 1250-1485.— Most of the inflexions of nouns and adjectives have in this period— between the middle of the thirteenth and the end of the fifteenth century— completely disappeared. The inflexions of verbs are also greatly reduced in number. The strong[1] mode of inflexion has ceased to be employed for verbs that are new-comers, and the weak mode has been adopted in its place. During the earlier part of this period, even country-people tried to speak French, and in this and other modes many French words found their way into English. A writer of the thirteenth century, John de Trevisa, says that country-people "fondeth [that is, try] with great bysynes for to speke Freynsch for to be more y-told of." The country-people did not succeed very well, as the ordinary proverb shows: "Jack would be a gentleman if he could speak French." Boys at school were expected to turn their Latin into French, and in the courts of law French only was allowed to be spoken. But in 1362 Edward III. gave his assent to an Act of Parliament allowing English to be used instead of Norman-French. "The yer of oure Lord," says John de Trevisa, "a thousond thre hondred foure score and fyve of the secunde Kyng Richard after the conquest, in al the gramer scoles of Engelond children leveth Freynsch, and construeth and turneth an Englysch." To the first half of this period belong a Metrical Chronicle, attributed to Robert of Gloucester; Langtoft's Metrical Chronicle, translated by Robert de Brunne; the Agenbite of Inwit, by Dan Michel of Northgate in Kent; and a few others. But to the second half belong the rich and varied productions of Geoffrey Chaucer, our first great poet and always one of our greatest writers; the alliterative poems of William Langley or Langlande; the more learned poems of John Gower; and the translation of the Bible and theological works of the reformer John Wyclif.

[1: See History of. Grammar]

7. Tudor English, 1485-1603.— Before the end of the sixteenth century almost all our inflexions had disappeared. The great dramatist Ben Jonson (1574-1637) laments the loss of the plural ending en for verbs, because wenten and hopen were much more musical and more useful in verse than went or hope; but its recovery was already past praying for. This period is remarkable for the introduction of an enormous number of Latin words, and this was due to the new interest taken in the literature of the Romans— an interest produced by what is called the Revival of Letters. But the most striking, as it is also the most important fact relating to this period, is the appearance of a group of dramatic writers, the greatest the world has ever seen. Chief among these was William Shakespeare. Of pure poetry perhaps the greatest writer was Edmund Spenser. The greatest prose-writer was Richard Hooker, and the pithiest Francis Bacon.

8. Modern English, 1603-1900.— The grammar of the language was fixed before this period, most of the accidence having entirely vanished. The vocabulary of the language, however, has gone on increasing, and is still increasing; for the English language, like the English people, is always ready to offer hospitality to all peaceful foreigners— words or human beings— that will land and settle within her coasts. And the tendency at the present time is not only to give a hearty welcome to newcomers from other lands, but to call back old words and old phrases that had been allowed to drop out of existence. Tennyson has been one of the chief agents in this happy restoration.

CHAPTER II.

THE HISTORY OF THE VOCABULARY OF THE ENGLISH LANGUAGE.

1. The English Nation.— The English people have for many centuries been the greatest travellers in the world. It was an Englishman— Francis Drake— who first went round the globe; and the English have colonised more foreign lands in every part of the world than any other people that ever existed. The English in this way have been influenced by the world without. But they have also been subjected to manifold influences from within— they have been exposed to greater political changes, and profounder though quieter political revolutions, than any other nation. In 1066 they were conquered by the Norman-French; and for several centuries they had French kings. Seeing and talking with many different peoples, they learned to adopt foreign words with ease, and to give them a home among the native-born words of the language. Trade is always a kindly and useful influence; and the trade of Great Britain has for many centuries been larger than that of any other nation. It has spread into every part of the world; it gives and receives from all tribes and nations, from every speech and tongue.

2. The English Element in English.— When the English came to this island in the fifth century, the number of words in the language they spoke was probably not over two thousand. Now, however, we possess a vocabulary of perhaps more than one hundred thousand words. And so eager and willing have we been to welcome foreign words, that it may be said with truth that: The majority of words in the English Tongue are not English. In fact, if we take the Latin language by itself, there are in our language more Latin words than English. But the grammar is distinctly English, and not Latin at all.

3. The Spoken Language and the Written Language— a Caution.— We must not forget what has been said about a language,— that it is not a printed thing— not a set of black marks upon paper, but that it is in truest truth a tongue or a speech. Hence we must be careful to distinguish between the spoken language and the written or printed language; between the language of the ear and the language of the eye; between the language of the mouth and the language of the dictionary; between the moving vocabulary of the market and the street, and the fixed vocabulary that has been catalogued and imprisoned in our dictionaries. If we can only keep this in view, we shall find that, though there are more Latin words in our vocabulary than English, the English words we possess are used in speaking a hundred times, or even a thousand times, oftener than the Latin words. It is the genuine English words that have life and movement; it is they that fly about in houses, in streets, and in markets; it is they that express with greatest force our truest and most usual sentiments— our inmost thoughts and our deepest feelings. Latin words are found often enough in books; but, when an English man or woman is deeply moved, he speaks pure

English and nothing else. Words are the coin of human intercourse; and it is the native coin of pure English with the native stamp that is in daily circulation.

4. A Diagram of English.— If we were to try to represent to the eye the proportions of the different elements in our vocabulary, as it is found in the dictionary, the diagram would take something like the following form:—

Diagram of the English Language.

———

ENGLISH WORDS.

———

LATIN WORDS
(including Norman-French, which are also Latin).

————

GREEK WORDS. Italian, Spanish, Portuguese, Dutch,
Hebrew, Arabic, Hindustani, Persian,
Malay, American, etc. etc.

————

5. The Foreign Elements in our English Vocabulary.— The different peoples and the different circumstances with which we have come in contact, have had many results— one among others, that of presenting us with contributions to our vocabulary. We found Kelts here; and hence we have a number of Keltic words in our vocabulary. The Romans held this island for several hundred years; and when they had to go in the year 410, they left behind them six Latin words, which we have inherited. In the seventh century, Augustine and his missionary monks from Rome brought over to us a larger number of Latin words; and the Church which they founded introduced ever more and more words from Rome. The Danes began to come over to this island in the eighth century; we had for some time a Danish dynasty seated on the throne of England: and hence we possess many Danish words. The Norman-French invasion in the eleventh century brought us many hundreds of Latin words; for French is in reality a branch of the Latin tongue. The Revival of Learning in the sixteenth century gave us several thousands of Latin words. And wherever our sailors and merchants have gone, they have brought back with them foreign words as well as foreign things— Arabic words from Arabia and Africa, Hindustani words from India, Persian words from Persia, Chinese words from China, and even Malay words from the peninsula of Malacca. Let us look a little more closely at these foreign elements.

6. The Keltic Element in English.— This element is of three kinds: (i) Those words which we received direct from the ancient Britons whom we found in the island; (ii) those which the Norman-French brought with them from Gaul; (iii) those which have lately come into the language from the Highlands of Scotland, or from Ireland, or from the writings of Sir Walter Scott.

7. The First Keltic Element.— This first contribution contains the following words: Breeches, clout, crock, cradle, darn, dainty, mop, pillow; barrow (a

funeral mound), glen, havoc, kiln, mattock, pool. It is worthy of note that the first eight in the list are the names of domestic— some even of kitchen— things and utensils. It may, perhaps, be permitted us to conjecture that in many cases the Saxon invader married a British wife, who spoke her own language, taught her children to speak their mother tongue, and whose words took firm root in the kitchen of the new English household. The names of most rivers, mountains, lakes, and hills are, of course, Keltic; for these names would not be likely to be changed by the English new-comers. There are two names for rivers which are found— in one form or another— in every part of Great Britain. These are the names Avon and Ex. The word Avon means simply water. We can conceive the children on a farm near a river speaking of it simply as "the water"; and hence we find fourteen Avons in this island. Ex also means water; and there are perhaps more than twenty streams in Great Britain with this name. The word appears as Ex in Exeter (the older and fuller form being Exanceaster— the camp on the Exe); as Ax in Axminster; as Ox in Oxford; as Ux in Uxbridge; and as Ouse in Yorkshire and other eastern counties. In Wales and Scotland, the hidden k changes its place and comes at the end. Thus in Wales we find Usk; and in Scotland, Esk. There are at least eight Esks in the kingdom of Scotland alone. The commonest Keltic name for a mountain is Pen or Ben (in Wales it is Pen; in Scotland the flatter form Ben is used). We find this word in England also under the form of Pennine; and, in Italy, as Apennine.

8. The Second Keltic Element.— The Normans came from Scandinavia early in the tenth century, and wrested the valley of the Seine out of the hands of Charles the Simple, the then king of the French. The language spoken by the people of France was a broken-down form of spoken Latin, which is now called French; but in this language they had retained many Gaulish words out of the old Gaulish language. Such are the words: Bag, bargain, barter; barrel, basin, basket, bucket; bonnet, button, ribbon; car, cart; dagger, gown; mitten, motley; rogue; varlet, vassal, wicket. The above words were brought over to Britain by the Normans; and they gradually took an acknowledged place among the words of our own language, and have held that place ever since.

9. The Third Keltic Element.— This consists of comparatively few words— such as clan; claymore (a sword); philabeg (a kind of kilt), kilt itself, brogue (a kind of shoe), plaid; pibroch (bagpipe war-music), slogan (a war-cry); and whisky. Ireland has given us shamrock, gag, log, clog, and brogue— in the sense of a mode of speech.

10. The Scandinavian Element in English.— Towards the end of the eighth century— in the year 787— the Teutons of the North, called Northmen, Normans, or Norsemen— but more commonly known as Danes— made their appearance on the eastern coast of Great Britain, and attacked the peaceful towns and quiet settlements of the English. These attacks became so frequent, and their occurrence was so much dreaded, that a prayer was inserted against them in a Litany of the time— "From the incursions of the Northmen, good Lord, deliver us!" In spite of the resistance of the English, the Danes had, before the end of the ninth century, succeeded in obtaining a permanent footing in

England; and, in the eleventh century, a Danish dynasty sat upon the English throne from the year 1016 to 1042. From the time of King Alfred, the Danes of the Danelagh were a settled part of the population of England; and hence we find, especially on the east coast, a large number of Danish names still in use.

11. Character of the Scandinavian Element.— The Northmen, as we have said, were Teutons; and they spoke a dialect of the great Teutonic (or German) language. The sounds of the Danish dialect— or language, as it must now be called— are harder than those of the German. We find a k instead of a ch; a p preferred to an f. The same is the case in Scotland, where the hard form kirk is preferred to the softer church. Where the Germans say Dorf— our English word Thorpe, a village— the Danes say Drup.

12. Scandinavian Words (i).— The words contributed to our language by the Scandinavians are of two kinds: (i) Names of places; and (ii) ordinary words. (i) The most striking instance of a Danish place-name is the noun by, a town. Mr Isaac Taylor[2] tells us that there are in the east of England more than six hundred names of towns ending in by. Almost all of these are found in the Danelagh, within the limits of the great highway made by the Romans to the north-west, and well-known as Watling Street. We find, for example, Whitby, or the town on the white cliffs; Grimsby, or the town of Grim, a great sea-rover, who obtained for his countrymen the right that all ships from the Baltic should come into the port of Grimsby free of duty; Tenby, that is Daneby; by-law, a law for a special town; and a vast number of others. The following Danish words also exist in our times— either as separate and individual words, or in composition— beck, a stream; fell, a hill or table-land; firth or fiord, an arm of the sea— the same as the Danish fiord; force, a waterfall; garth, a yard or enclosure; holm, an island in a river; kirk, a church; oe, an island; thorpe, a village; thwaite, a forest clearing; and vik or wick, a station for ships, or a creek.

[2: Words and Places]

13. Scandinavian Words (ii).— The most useful and the most frequently employed word that we have received from the Danes is the word are. The pure English word for this is beoth or sindon. The Danes gave us also the habit of using to before an infinitive. Their word for to was at; and at still survives and is in use in Lincolnshire. We find also the following Danish words in our language: blunt, bole (of a tree), bound (on a journey— properly boun), busk (to dress), cake, call, crop (to cut), curl, cut, dairy, daze, din, droop, fellow, flit, for, froward, hustings, ill, irk, kid, kindle, loft, odd, plough, root, scold, sky, tarn (a small mountain lake), weak, and ugly. It is in Northumberland, Durham, Yorkshire, Lincoln, Norfolk, and even in the western counties of Cumberland and Lancashire, that we find the largest admixture of Scandinavian words.

14. Influence of the Scandinavian Element.— The introduction of the Danes and the Danish language into England had the result, in the east, of unsettling the inflexions of our language, and thus of preparing the way for their complete disappearance. The declensions of nouns became unsettled; nouns that used to make their plural in a or in u took the more striking plural suffix as that belonged to a quite different declension. The same things happened to

adjectives, verbs, and other parts of language. The causes of this are not far to seek. Spoken language can never be so accurate as written language; the mass of the English and Danes never cared or could care much for grammar; and both parties to a conversation would of course hold firmly to the root of the word, which was intelligible to both of them, and let the inflexions slide, or take care of themselves. The more the English and Danes mixed with each other, the oftener they met at church, at games, and in the market-place, the more rapidly would this process of stripping go on,— the smaller care would both peoples take of the grammatical inflexions which they had brought with them into this country.

15. The Latin Element in English.— So far as the number of words— the vocabulary— of the language is concerned, the Latin contribution is by far the most important element in our language. Latin was the language of the Romans; and the Romans at one time were masters of the whole known world. No wonder, then, that they influenced so many peoples, and that their language found its way— east and west, and south and north— into almost all the countries of Europe. There are, as we have seen, more Latin than English words in our own language; and it is therefore necessary to make ourselves acquainted with the character and the uses of the Latin element— an element so important— in English.[3] Not only have the Romans made contributions of large numbers of words to the English language, but they have added to it a quite new quality, and given to its genius new powers of expression. So true is this, that we may say— without any sense of unfairness, or any feeling of exaggeration— that, until the Latin element was thoroughly mixed, united with, and transfused into the original English, the writings of Shakespeare were impossible, the poetry of the sixteenth and seventeenth centuries could not have come into existence. This is true of Shakespeare; and it is still more true of Milton. His most powerful poetical thoughts are written in lines, the most telling words in which are almost always Latin. This may be illustrated by the following lines from "Lycidas":—

"It was that fatal and perfidious bark,
Built in the eclipse, and rigged with curses dark,
That sunk so low that sacred head of thine!"

[3: In the last half of this sentence, all the essential
words— necessary, acquainted, character, uses, element,
important, are Latin (except character, which is Greek).]

16. The Latin Contributions and their Dates.— The first contribution of Latin words was made by the Romans— not, however, to the English, but to the Britons. The Romans held this island from A.D. 43 to A.D. 410. They left behind them— when they were obliged to go— a small contribution of six words— six only, but all of them important. The second contribution— to a large extent ecclesiastical— was made by Augustine and his missionary monks from Rome, and their visit took place in the year 596. The third contribution

was made through the medium of the Norman-French, who seized and subdued this island in the year 1066 and following years. The fourth contribution came to us by the aid of the Revival of Learning— rather a process than an event, the dates of which are vague, but which may be said to have taken place in the sixteenth and seventeenth centuries. The Latin left for us by the Romans is called Latin of the First Period; that brought over by the missionaries from Rome, Latin of the Second Period; that given us by the Norman-French, Latin of the Third Period; and that which came to us from the Revival of Learning, Latin of the Fourth Period. The first consists of a few names handed down to us through the Britons; the second, of a number of words— mostly relating to ecclesiastical affairs— brought into the spoken language by the monks; the third, of a large vocabulary, that came to us by mouth and ear; and the fourth, of a very large treasure of words, which we received by means of books and the eye. Let us now look more closely and carefully at them, each in its turn.

17. Latin of the First Period (i).— The Romans held Britain for nearly four hundred years; and they succeeded in teaching the wealthier classes among the Southern Britons to speak Latin. They also built towns in the island, made splendid roads, formed camps at important points, framed good laws, and administered the affairs of the island with considerable justice and uprightness. But, never having come directly into contact with the Angles or Saxons themselves, they could not in any way influence their language by oral communication— by speaking to them. What they left behind them was only six words, most of which became merely the prefixes or the suffixes of the names of places. These six words were Castra, a camp; Strata (via), a paved road; Colonia, a settlement (generally of soldiers); Fossa, a trench; Portus, a harbour; and Vallum, a rampart.

18. Latin of the First Period (ii).— (a) The treatment of the Latin word castra in this island has been both singular and significant. It has existed in this country for nearly nineteen hundred years; and it has always taken the colouring of the locality into whose soil it struck root. In the north and east of England it is sounded hard, and takes the form of caster, as in Lancaster, Doncaster, Tadcaster, and others. In the midland counties, it takes the softer form of cester, as in Leicester, Towcester; and in the extreme west and south, it takes the still softer form of chester, as in Chester, Manchester, Winchester, and others. It is worthy of notice that there are in Scotland no words ending in caster. Though the Romans had camps in Scotland, they do not seem to have been so important as to become the centres of towns. (b) The word strata has also taken different forms in different parts of England. While castra has always been a suffix, strata shows itself constantly as a prefix. When the Romans came to this island, the country was impassable by man. There were no roads worthy of the name,— what paths there were being merely foot-paths or bridle-tracks. One of the first things the Romans did was to drive a strongly built military road from Richborough, near Dover, to the river Dee, on which they formed a standing camp (Castra stativa) which to this day bears the name of Chester. This great road became the highway of all travellers from north to south,— was known as

"The Street," and was called by the Saxons Watling Street. But this word street also became a much-used prefix, and took the different forms of strat, strad, stret, and streat. All towns with such names are to be found on this or some other great Roman road. Thus we have Stratford-on-Avon, Stratton, Stradbroke, Stretton, Stretford (near Manchester), and Streatham (near London). —Over the other words we need not dwell so long. Colonia we find in Colne, Lincoln, and others; fossa in Fossway, Fosbrooke, and Fosbridge; portus, in Portsmouth, and Bridport; and vallum in the words wall, bailey, and bailiff. The Normans called the two courts in front of their castles the inner and outer baileys; and the officer in charge of them was called the bailiff.

19. Latin Element of the Second Period (i).— The story of Pope Gregory and the Roman mission to England is widely known. Gregory, when a young man, was crossing the Roman forum one morning, and, when passing the side where the slave-mart was held, observed, as he walked, some beautiful boys, with fair hair, blue eyes, and clear bright complexion. He asked a bystander of what nation the boys were. The answer was, that they were Angles. "No, not Angles," he replied; "they are angels." On learning further that they were heathens, he registered a silent vow that he would, if Providence gave him an opportunity, deliver them from the darkness of heathendom, and bring them and their relatives into the light and liberty of the Gospel. Time passed by; and in the long course of time Gregory became Pope. In his unlooked-for greatness, he did not forget his vow. In the year 596 he sent over to Kent a missionary, called Augustine, along with forty monks. They were well received by the King of Kent, allowed to settle in Canterbury, and to build a small cathedral there.

20. Latin Element of the Second Period (ii).— This mission, the churches that grew out of it, the Christian customs that in time took root in the country, and the trade that followed in its track, brought into the language a number of Latin words, most of them the names of church offices, services, and observances. Thus we find, in our oldest English, the words, postol from apostolus, a person sent; biscop, from episcopus, an overseer; calc, from calix, a cup; clerc, from clericus, an ordained member of the church; munec, from mon[)a]chus, a solitary person or monk; preost, from presbyter, an elder; aelmesse, from ele[-e]mos[)u]n[-e], alms; predician, from prædicare, to preach; regol, from regula, a rule. (Apostle, bishop, clerk, monk, priest, and alms come to us really from Greek words— but through the Latin tongue.)

21. Latin Element of the Second Period (iii).— The introduction of the Roman form of Christianity brought with it increased communication with Rome and with the Continent generally; widened the experience of Englishmen; gave a stimulus to commerce; and introduced into this island new things and products, and along with the things and products new names. To this period belongs the introduction of the words: Butter, cheese; cedar, fig, pear, peach; lettuce, lily; pepper, pease; camel, lion, elephant; oyster, trout; pound, ounce; candle, table; marble; mint.

22. Latin of the Third Period (i).— The Latin element of the Third Period is in reality the French that was brought over to this island by the Normans in

1066, and is generally called Norman-French. It differed from the French of Paris both in spelling and in pronunciation. For example, Norman-French wrote people for peuple; léal for loyal; réal for royal; réalm for royaume; and so on. But both of these dialects (and every dialect of French) are simply forms of Latin— not of the Latin written and printed in books, but of the Latin spoken in the camp, the fields, the streets, the village, and the cottage. The Romans conquered Gaul, where a Keltic tongue was spoken; and the Gauls gradually adopted Latin as their mother tongue, and— with the exception of the Brétons of Brittany— left off their Keltic speech almost entirely. In adopting the Latin tongue, they had— as in similar cases— taken firm hold of the root of the word, but changed the pronunciation of it, and had, at the same time, compressed very much or entirely dropped many of the Latin inflexions. The French people, an intermixture of Gauls and other tribes (some of them, like the Franks, German), ceased, in fact, to speak their own language, and learned the Latin tongue. The Norsemen, led by Duke Rolf or Rollo or Rou, marched south in large numbers; and, in the year 912, wrested from King Charles the Simple the fair valley of the Seine, settled in it, and gave to it the name of Normandy. These Norsemen, now Normans, were Teutons, and spoke a Teutonic dialect; but, when they settled in France, they learned in course of time to speak French. The kind of French they spoke is called Norman-French, and it was this kind of French that they brought over with them in 1066. But Norman-French had made its appearance in England before the famous year of '66; for Edward the Confessor, who succeeded to the English throne in 1042, had been educated at the Norman Court; and he not only spoke the language himself, but insisted on its being spoken by the nobles who lived with him in his Court.

23. Latin of the Third Period (ii). Chief Dates. —The Normans, having utterly beaten down the resistance of the English, seized the land and all the political power of this country, and filled all kinds of offices— both spiritual and temporal— with their Norman brethren. Norman-French became the language of the Court and the nobility, the language of Parliament and the law courts, of the universities and the schools, of the Church and of literature. The English people held fast to their own tongue; but they picked up many French words in the markets and other places "where men most do congregate." But French, being the language of the upper and ruling classes, was here and there learned by the English or Saxon country-people who had the ambition to be in the fashion, and were eager "to speke Frensch, for to be more y-told of,"— to be more highly considered than their neighbours. It took about three hundred years for French words and phrases to soak thoroughly into English; and it was not until England was saturated with French words and French rhythms that the great poet Chaucer appeared to produce poetic narratives that were read with delight both by Norman baron and by Saxon yeoman. In the course of these three hundred years this intermixture of French with English had been slowly and silently going on. Let us look at a few of the chief land-marks in the long process. In 1042 Edward the Confessor introduces Norman-French into his Court. In 1066 Duke William introduces Norman-French into the whole

country, and even into parts of Scotland. The oldest English, or Anglo-Saxon, ceases to be written, anywhere in the island, in public documents, in the year 1154. In 1204 we lost Normandy, a loss that had the effect of bringing the English and the Normans closer together. Robert of Gloucester writes his chronicle in 1272, and uses a large number of French words. But, as early as the reign of Henry the Third, in the year 1258, the reformed and reforming Government of the day issued a proclamation in English, as well as in French and Latin. In 1303, Robert of Brunn introduces a large number of French words. The French wars in Edward the Third's reign brought about a still closer union of the Norman and the Saxon elements of the nation. But, about the middle of the fourteenth century a reaction set in, and it seemed as if the genius of the English language refused to take in any more French words. The English silent stubbornness seemed to have prevailed, and Englishmen had made up their minds to be English in speech, as they were English to the backbone in everything else. Norman-French had, in fact, become provincial, and was spoken only here and there. Before the great Plague— commonly spoken of as "The Black Death"— of 1349, both high and low seemed to be alike bent on learning French, but the reaction may be said to date from this year. The culminating point of this reaction may perhaps be seen in an Act of Parliament passed in 1362 by Edward III., by which both French and Latin had to give place to English in our courts of law. The poems of Chaucer are the literary result— "the bright consummate flower" of the union of two great powers— the brilliance of the French language on the one hand and the homely truth and steadfastness of English on the other. Chaucer was born in 1340, and died in 1400; so that we may say that he and his poems— though not the causes— are the signs and symbols of the great influence that French obtained and held over our mother tongue. But although we accepted so many words from our Norman-French visitors and immigrants, we accepted from them no habit of speech whatever. We accepted from them no phrase or idiom: the build and nature of the English language remained the same— unaffected by foreign manners or by foreign habits. It is true that Chaucer has the ridiculous phrase, "I n'am but dead" (for "I am quite dead"[4])— which is a literal translation of the well-known French idiom, "Je ne suis que." But, though our tongue has always been and is impervious to foreign idiom, it is probably owing to the great influx of French words which took place chiefly in the thirteenth century that many people have acquired a habit of using a long French or Latin word when an English word would do quite as well— or, indeed, a great deal better. Thus some people are found to call a good house, a desirable mansion; and, instead of the quiet old English proverb, "Buy once, buy twice," we have the roundabout Latinisms, "A single commission will ensure a repetition of orders." An American writer, speaking of the foreign ambassadors who had been attacked by Japanese soldiers in Yeddo, says that "they concluded to occupy a location more salubrious." This is only a foreign language, instead of the simple and homely English: "They made up their minds to settle in a healthier spot."

[4: Or, as an Irishman would say, "I am kilt entirely."]

24. Latin of the Third Period (iii). Norman Words (a). —The Norman-French words were of several different kinds. There were words connected with war, with feudalism, and with the chase. There were new law terms, and words connected with the State, and the new institutions introduced by the Normans. There were new words brought in by the Norman churchmen. New titles unknown to the English were also introduced. A better kind of cooking, a higher and less homely style of living, was brought into this country by the Normans; and, along with these, new and unheard-of words.

25. Norman Words (b).— The following are some of the Norman-French terms connected with war: Arms, armour; assault, battle; captain, chivalry; joust, lance; standard, trumpet; mail, vizor. The English word for armour was harness; but the Normans degraded that word into the armour of a horse. Battle comes from the Fr. battre, to beat: the corresponding English word is fight. Captain comes from the Latin caput, a head. Mail comes from the Latin macula, the mesh of a net; and the first coats of mail were made of rings or a kind of metal network. Vizor comes from the Fr. viser, to look. It was the barred part of the helmet which a man could see through.

26. Norman Words (c).— Feudalism may be described as the holding of land on condition of giving or providing service in war. Thus a knight held land of his baron, under promise to serve him so many days; a baron of his king, on condition that he brought so many men into the field for such and such a time at the call of his Overlord. William the Conqueror made the feudal system universal in every part of England, and compelled every English baron to swear homage to himself personally. Words relating to feudalism are, among others: Homage, fealty; esquire, vassal; herald, scutcheon, and others. Homage is the declaration of obedience for life of one man to another— that the inferior is the man (Fr. homme; L. homo) of the superior. Fealty is the Norman-French form of the word fidelity. An esquire is a scutiger (L.), or shield-bearer; for he carried the shield of the knight, when they were travelling and no fighting was going on. A vassal was a "little young man,"— in Low-Latin vassallus, a diminutive of vassus, from the Keltic word gwâs, a man. (The form vassaletus is also found, which gives us our varlet and valet.) Scutcheon comes from the Lat. scutum, a shield. Then scutcheon or escutcheon came to mean coat-of-arms— or the marks and signs on his shield by which the name and family of a man were known, when he himself was covered from head to foot in iron mail.

27. Norman Words (d).— The terms connected with the chase are: Brace, couple; chase, course; covert, copse, forest; leveret, mews; quarry, venison. A few remarks about some of these may be interesting. Brace comes from the Old French brace, an arm (Mod. French bras); from the Latin brachium. The root-idea seems to be that which encloses or holds up. Thus bracing air is that which strings up the nerves and muscles; and a brace of birds was two birds tied together with a string. —The word forest contains in itself a good deal of unwritten Norman history. It comes from the Latin adverb foras, out of doors. Hence, in Italy, a stranger or foreigner is still called a forestiere. A forest in Norman-French was not necessarily a breadth of land covered with trees; it was

simply land out of the jurisdiction of the common law. Hence, when William the Conqueror created the New Forest, he merely took the land out of the rule and charge of the common law, and put it under his own regal power and personal care. In land of this kind— much of which was kept for hunting in— trees were afterwards planted, partly to shelter large game, and partly to employ ground otherwise useless in growing timber. —Mews is a very odd word. It comes from the Latin verb mutare, to change. When the falcons employed in hunting were changing their feathers, or moulting (the word moult is the same as mews in a different dress), the French shut them in a cage, which they called mue— from mutare. Then the stables for horses were put in the same place; and hence a row of stables has come to be called a mews. —Quarry is quite as strange. The word quarry, which means a mine of stones, comes from the Latin quadr[-a]re, to make square. But the hunting term quarry is of a quite different origin. That comes from the Latin cor (the heart), which the Old French altered into quer. When a wild beast was run down and killed, the heart and entrails were thrown to the dogs as their share of the hunt. Hence Milton says of the eagle, "He scents his quarry from afar." —The word venison comes to us, through French, from the Lat. ven[-a]ri, to hunt; and hence it means hunted flesh. The same word gives us venery— the term that was used in the fourteenth century, by Chaucer among others, for hunting.

28. Norman Words (e).— The Normans introduced into England their own system of law, their own law officers; and hence, into the English language, came Norman-French law terms. The following are a few: Assize, attorney; chancellor, court; judge, justice; plaintiff, sue; summons, trespass. A few remarks about some of these may be useful. The chancellor (cancellarius) was the legal authority who sat behind lattice-work, which was called in Latin cancelli. This word means, primarily, little crabs; and it is a diminutive from cancer, a crab. It was so called because the lattice-work looked like crabs' claws crossed. Our word cancel comes from the same root: it means to make cross lines through anything we wish deleted. —Court comes from the Latin cors or cohors, a sheep-pen. It afterwards came to mean an enclosure, and also a body of Roman soldiers. —The proper English word for a judge is deemster or demster (which appears as the proper name Dempster); and this is still the name for a judge in the Isle of Man. The French word comes from two Latin words, dico, I utter, and jus, right. The word jus is seen in the other French term which we have received from the Normans— justice. —Sue comes from the Old Fr. suir, which appears in Modern Fr. as suivre. It is derived from the Lat. word sequor, I follow (which gives our sequel); and we have compounds of it in ensue, issue, and pursue. —The tres in trespass is a French form of the Latin trans, beyond or across. Trespass, therefore, means to cross the bounds of right.

29. Norman Words (f).— Some of the church terms introduced by the Norman-French are: Altar, Bible; baptism, ceremony; friar; tonsure; penance, relic. —The Normans gave us the words title and dignity themselves, and also the following titles: Duke, marquis; count, viscount; peer; mayor, and others. A duke is a leader; from the Latin dux (= duc-s). A marquis is a lord who has to

ride the marches or borders between one county, or between one country, and another. A marquis was also called a Lord-Marcher. The word count never took root in this island, because its place was already occupied by the Danish name earl; but we preserve it in the names countess and viscount— the latter of which means a person in the place of (L. vice) a count. Peer comes from the Latin par, an equal. The House of Peers is the House of Lords— that is, of those who are, at least when in the House, equal in rank and equal in power of voting. It is a fundamental doctrine in English law that every man "is to be tried by his peers." —It is worthy of note that, in general, the French names for different kinds of food designated the cooked meats; while the names for the living animals that furnish them are English. Thus we have beef and ox; mutton and sheep; veal and calf; pork and pig. There is a remarkable passage in Sir Walter Scott's 'Ivanhoe,' which illustrates this fact with great force and picturesqueness:—

"'Gurth, I advise thee to call off Fangs, and leave the herd to their destiny, which, whether they meet with bands of travelling soldiers, or of outlaws, or of wandering pilgrims, can be little else than to be converted into Normans before morning, to thy no small ease and comfort.'

"'The swine turned Normans to my comfort!' quoth Gurth; 'expound that to me, Wamba, for my brain is too dull, and my mind too vexed, to read riddles.'

"'Why, how call you those grunting brutes running about on their four legs?' demanded Wamba.

"'Swine, fool, swine,' said the herd; 'every fool knows that.'

"'And swine is good Saxon,' said the jester; 'but how call you the sow when she is flayed, and drawn, and quartered, and hung up by the heels, like a traitor?'

"'Pork,' answered the swine-herd.

"'I am very glad every fool knows that too,' said Wamba; 'and pork, I think, is good Norman-French: and so when the brute lives, and is in the charge of a Saxon slave, she goes by her Saxon name; but becomes a Norman, and is called pork, when she is carried to the castle-hall to feast among the nobles; what dost thou think of this, friend Gurth, ha?'

"'It is but too true doctrine, friend Wamba, however it got into thy fool's pate.'

"'Nay, I can tell you more,' said Wamba, in the same tone; 'there is old Alderman Ox continues to hold his Saxon epithet, while he is under the charge of serfs and bondsmen such as thou, but becomes Beef, a fiery French gallant, when he arrives before the worshipful jaws that are destined to consume him. Myhneer Calf, too, becomes Monsieur de Veau in the like manner; he is Saxon when he requires tendance, and takes a Norman name when he becomes matter of enjoyment.'"

30. General Character of the Norman-French Contributions.— The Norman-French contributions to our language gave us a number of general names or class-names; while the names for individual things are, in general, of purely English origin. The words animal and beast, for example, are French (or Latin); but the words fox, hound, whale, snake, wasp, and fly are purely English. —The words family, relation, parent, ancestor, are French; but the names father,

mother, son, daughter, gossip, are English. —The words title and dignity are French; but the words king and queen, lord and lady, knight and sheriff, are English. —Perhaps the most remarkable instance of this is to be found in the abstract terms employed for the offices and functions of State. Of these, the English language possesses only one— the word kingdom. Norman-French, on the other hand, has given us the words realm, court, state, constitution, people, treaty, audience, navy, army, and others— amounting in all to nearly forty. When, however, we come to terms denoting labour and work— such as agriculture and seafaring, we find the proportions entirely reversed. The English language, in such cases, contributes almost everything; the French nearly nothing. In agriculture, while plough, rake, harrow, flail, and many others are English words, not a single term for an agricultural process or implement has been given us by the warlike Norman-French. —While the words ship and boat; hull and fleet; oar and sail, are all English, the Normans have presented us with only the single word prow. It is as if all the Norman conqueror had to do was to take his stand at the prow, gazing upon the land he was going to seize, while the Low-German sailors worked for him at oar and sail. —Again, while the names of the various parts of the body— eye, nose, cheek, tongue, hand, foot, and more than eighty others— are all English, we have received only about ten similar words from the French— such as spirit and corpse; perspiration; face and stature. Speaking broadly, we may say that all words that express general notions, or generalisations, are French or Latin; while words that express specific actions or concrete existences are pure English. Mr Spalding observes— "We use a foreign term naturalised when we speak of 'colour' universally; but we fall back on our home stores if we have to tell what the colour is, calling it 'red' or 'yellow,' 'white' or 'black,' 'green' or 'brown.' We are Romans when we speak in a general way of 'moving'; but we are Teutons if we 'leap' or 'spring,' if we 'slip,' 'slide,' or 'fall,' if we 'walk,' 'run,' 'swim,' or 'ride,' if we 'creep' or 'crawl' or 'fly.'"

31. Gains to English from Norman-French.— The gains from the Norman-French contribution are large, and are also of very great importance. Mr Lowell says, that the Norman element came in as quickening leaven to the rather heavy and lumpy Saxon dough. It stirred the whole mass, gave new life to the language, a much higher and wider scope to the thoughts, much greater power and copiousness to the expression of our thoughts, and a finer and brighter rhythm to our English sentences. "To Chaucer," he says, in 'My Study Windows,' "French must have been almost as truly a mother tongue as English. In him we see the first result of the Norman yeast upon the home-baked Saxon loaf. The flour had been honest, the paste well kneaded, but the inspiring leaven was wanting till the Norman brought it over. Chaucer works still in the solid material of his race, but with what airy lightness has he not infused it? Without ceasing to be English, he has escaped from being insular." Let us look at some of these gains a little more in detail.

32. Norman-French Synonyms.— We must not consider a synonym as a word that means exactly the same thing as the word of which it is a synonym;

because then there would be neither room nor use for such a word in the language. A synonym is a word of the same meaning as another, but with a slightly different shade of meaning,— or it is used under different circumstances and in a different connection, or it puts the same idea under a new angle. Begin and commence, will and testament, are exact equivalents— are complete synonyms; but there are very few more of this kind in our language. The moment the genius of a language gets hold of two words of the same meaning, it sets them to do different kinds of work,— to express different parts or shades of that meaning. Thus limb and member, luck and fortune, have the same meaning; but we cannot speak of a limb of the Royal Society, or of the luck of the Rothschilds, who made their fortune by hard work and steady attention to business. We have, by the aid of the Norman-French contributions, flower as well as bloom; branch and bough; purchase and buy; amiable and friendly; cordial and hearty; country and land; gentle and mild; desire and wish; labour and work; miserable and wretched. These pairs of words enable poets and other writers to use the right word in the right place. And we, preferring our Saxon or good old English words to any French or Latin importations, prefer to speak of a hearty welcome instead of a cordial reception; of a loving wife instead of an amiable consort; of a wretched man instead of a miserable individual.

33. Bilingualism.— How did these Norman-French words find their way into the language? What was the road by which they came? What was the process that enabled them to find a place in and to strike deep root into our English soil? Did the learned men— the monks and the clergy— make a selection of words, write them in their books, and teach them to the English people? Nothing of the sort. The process was a much ruder one— but at the same time one much more practical, more effectual, and more lasting in its results. The two peoples— the Normans and the English— found that they had to live together. They met at church, in the market-place, in the drilling field, at the archery butts, in the courtyards of castles; and, on the battle-fields of France, the Saxon bowman showed that he could fight as well, as bravely, and even to better purpose than his lord— the Norman baron. At all these places, under all these circumstances, the Norman and the Englishman were obliged to speak with each other. Now arose a striking phenomenon. Every man, as Professor Earle puts it, turned himself as it were into a walking phrase-book or dictionary. When a Norman had to use a French word, he tried to put the English word for it alongside of the French word; when an Englishman used an English word, he joined with it the French equivalent. Then the language soon began to swarm with "yokes of words"; our words went in couples; and the habit then begun has continued down even to the present day. And thus it is that we possess such couples as will and testament; act and deed; use and wont; aid and abet. Chaucer's poems are full of these pairs. He joins together hunting and venery (though both words mean exactly the same thing); nature and kind; cheere and face; pray and beseech; mirth and jollity. Later on, the Prayer-Book, which was written in the years 1540 to 1559, keeps up the habit: and we find the pairs acknowledge and confess; assemble and meet together; dissemble and cloak;

humble and lowly. To the more English part of the congregation the simple Saxon words would come home with kindly association; to others, the words confess, assemble, dissemble, and humble would speak with greater force and clearness. —Such is the phenomenon called by Professor Earle bilingualism. "It is, in fact," he says, "a putting of colloquial formulæ to do the duty of a French-English and English-French vocabulary." Even Hooker, who wrote at the end of the sixteenth century, seems to have been obliged to use these pairs; and we find in his writings the couples "cecity and blindness," "nocive and hurtful," "sense and meaning."

34. Losses of English from the Incoming of Norman-French.— (i) Before the coming of the Normans, the English language was in the habit of forming compounds with ease and effect. But, after the introduction of the Norman-French language, that power seems gradually to have disappeared; and ready-made French or Latin words usurped the place of the home-grown English compound. Thus despair pushed out wanhope; suspicion dethroned wantrust; bidding-sale was expelled by auction; learning-knight by disciple; rime-craft by the Greek word arithmetic; gold-hoard by treasure; book-hoard by library; earth-tilth by agriculture; wonstead by residence; and so with a large number of others. —Many English words, moreover, had their meanings depreciated and almost degraded; and the words themselves lost their ancient rank and dignity. Thus the Norman conquerors put their foot— literally and metaphorically— on the Saxon chair,[5] which thus became a stool, or a footstool. Thatch, which is a doublet of the word deck, was the name for any kind of roof; but the coming of the Norman-French lowered it to indicate a roof of straw. Whine was used for the weeping or crying of human beings; but it is now restricted to the cry of a dog. Hide was the generic term for the skin of any animal; it is now limited in modern English to the skin of a beast. —The most damaging result upon our language was that it entirely stopped the growth of English words. We could, for example, make out of the word burn— the derivatives brunt, brand, brandy, brown, brimstone, and others; but this power died out with the coming in of the Norman-French language. After that, instead of growing our own words, we adopted them ready-made. —Professor Craik compares the English and Latin languages to two banks; and says that, when the Normans came over, the account at the English bank was closed, and we drew only upon the Latin bank. But the case is worse than this. English lost its power of growth and expansion from the centre; from this time, it could only add to its bulk by borrowing and conveying from without— by the external accretion of foreign words.

[5: Chair is the Norman-French form of the French chaise. The Germans still call a chair a stuhl; and among the English, stool was the universal name till the twelfth century.]

35. Losses of English from the Incoming of Norman-French.— (ii) The arrestment of growth in the purely English part of our language, owing to the irruption of Norman-French, and also to the ease with which we could take a

ready-made word from Latin or from Greek, killed off an old power which we once possessed, and which was not without its own use and expressiveness. This was the power of making compound words. The Greeks in ancient times had, and the Germans in modern times have, this power in a high degree. Thus a Greek comic poet has a word of fourteen syllables, which may be thus translated—

"Meanly-rising-early-and-hurrying-to-the-tribunal-
to-denounce-another-for-an-infraction-of-the-law-
concerning-the-exportation-of-figs."[6]

And the Germans have a compound like "the-all-to-nothing-crushing philosopher." The Germans also say iron-path for railway, handshoe for glove, and finger-hat for thimble. We also possessed this power at one time, and employed it both in proper and in common names. Thus we had and have the names Brakespear, Shakestaff, Shakespear, Golightly, Dolittle, Standfast; and the common nouns want-wit, find-fault, mumble-news (for tale-bearer), pinch-penny (for miser), slugabed. In older times we had three-foot-stool, three-man-beetle[7]; stone-cold, heaven-bright, honey-sweet, snail-slow, nut-brown, lily-livered (for cowardly); brand-fire-new; earth-wandering, wind-dried, thunder-blasted, death-doomed, and many others. But such words as forbears or fore-elders have been pushed out by ancestors; forewit by caution or prudence; and inwit by conscience. Mr Barnes, the Dorsetshire poet, would like to see these and similar compounds restored, and thinks that we might well return to the old clear well-springs of "English undefiled," and make our own compounds out of our own words. He even carries his desires into the region of English grammar, and, for degrees of comparison, proposes the phrase pitches of suchness. Thus, instead of the Latin word omnibus, he would have folk-wain; for the Greek botany, he would substitute wort-lore; for auction, he would give us bode-sale; globule he would replace with ballkin; the Greek word horizon must give way to the pure English sky-edge; and, instead of quadrangle, he would have us all write and say four-winkle.

[6: In two words, a fig-shower or sycophant.]

[7: A club for beating clothes, that could be handled only by three men.]

36. Losses of English from the Incoming of Norman-French.— (iii) When once a way was made for the entrance of French words into our English language, the immigrations were rapid and numerous. Hence there were many changes both in the grammar and in the vocabulary of English from the year 1100, the year in which we may suppose those Englishmen who were living at the date of the battle of Hastings had died out. These changes were more or less rapid, according to circumstances. But perhaps the most rapid and remarkable change took place in the lifetime of William Caxton, the great printer, who was born in 1410. In his preface to his translation of the 'Æneid' of Virgil, which he published in 1490, when he was eighty years of age, he says that he cannot understand old books that were written when he was a boy— that "the olde

Englysshe is more lyke to dutche than englysshe," and that "our langage now vsed varyeth ferre from that whiche was vsed and spoken when I was borne. For we Englysshemen ben borne ynder the domynacyon of the mone [moon], which is neuer stedfaste, but euer wauerynge, wexynge one season, and waneth and dycreaseth another season." This as regards time. —But he has the same complaint to make as regards place. "Comyn englysshe that is spoken in one shyre varyeth from another." And he tells an odd story in illustration of this fact. He tells about certain merchants who were in a ship "in Tamyse" (on the Thames), who were bound for Zealand, but were wind-stayed at the Foreland, and took it into their heads to go on shore there. One of the merchants, whose name was Sheffelde, a mercer, entered a house, "and axed for mete, and specyally he axyd after eggys." But the "goode-wyf" replied that she "coude speke no frenshe." The merchant, who was a steady Englishman, lost his temper, "for he also coude speke no frenshe, but wolde have hadde eggys; and she understode hym not." Fortunately, a friend happened to join him in the house, and he acted as interpreter. The friend said that "he wolde have eyren; then the goode wyf sayde that she understod hym wel." And then the simple-minded but much-perplexed Caxton goes on to say: "Loo! what sholde a man in thyse dayes now wryte, eggës or eyren?" Such were the difficulties that beset printers and writers in the close of the fifteenth century.

37. Latin of the Fourth Period.— (i) This contribution differs very essentially in character from the last. The Norman-French contribution was a gift from a people to a people— from living beings to living beings; this new contribution was rather a conveyance of words from books to books, and it never influenced— in any great degree— the spoken language of the English people. The ear and the mouth carried the Norman-French words into our language; the eye, the pen, and the printing-press were the instruments that brought in the Latin words of the Fourth Period. The Norman-French words that came in took and kept their place in the spoken language of the masses of the people; the Latin words that we received in the sixteenth and seventeenth centuries kept their place in the written or printed language of books, of scholars, and of literary men. These new Latin words came in with the Revival of Learning, which is also called the Renascence.

The Turks attacked and took Constantinople in the year 1453; and the great Greek and Latin scholars who lived in that city hurriedly packed up their priceless manuscripts and books, and fled to all parts of Italy, Germany, France, and even into England. The loss of the East became the gain of the West. These scholars became teachers; they taught the Greek and Roman classics to eager and earnest learners; and thus a new impulse was given to the study of the great masterpieces of human thought and literary style. And so it came to pass in course of time that every one who wished to become an educated man studied the literature of Greece and Rome. Even women took to the study. Lady Jane Grey was a good Greek and Latin scholar; and so was Queen Elizabeth. From this time began an enormous importation of Latin words into our language. Being imported by the eye and the pen, they suffered little or no change; the spirit of the people did not influence them in the least— neither the organs of speech nor the ear affected either the pronunciation or the spelling of them. If we look down the columns of any English dictionary, we shall find these later Latin words in hundreds. Opinionem became opinion; factionem, faction; orationem, oration; pungentem passed over in the form of pungent (though we had poignant already from the French); pauperem came in as pauper; and separatum became separate.

38. Latin of the Fourth Period.— (ii) This went on to such an extent in the sixteenth and the beginning of the seventeenth century, that one writer says of those who spoke and wrote this Latinised English, "If some of their mothers were alive, they were not able to tell what they say." And Sir Thomas Browne (1605-1682) remarks: "If elegancy (= the use of Latin words) still proceedeth, and English pens maintain that stream we have of late observed to flow from many, we shall, within a few years, be fain to learn Latin to understand English, and a work will prove of equal facility in either." Mr Alexander Gill, an eminent schoolmaster, and the then head-master of St Paul's School, where, among his other pupils, he taught John Milton, wrote a book in 1619 on the English language; and, among other remarks, he says: "O harsh lips! I now hear all around me such words as common, vices, envy, malice; even virtue, study, justice, pity, mercy, compassion, profit, commodity, colour, grace, favour, acceptance. But whither, I pray, in all the world, have you banished those words which our forefathers used for these new-fangled ones? Are our words to be executed like our citizens?" And he calls this fashion of using Latin words "the new mange in our speaking and writing." But the fashion went on growing; and even uneducated people thought it a clever thing to use a Latin instead of a good English word. Samuel Rowlands, a writer in the seventeenth century, ridicules this affectation in a few lines of verse. He pretends that he was out walking on the highroad, and met a countryman who wanted to know what o'clock it was, and whether he was on the right way to the town or village he was making for. The writer saw at once that he was a simple bumpkin; and, when he heard that he had lost his way, he turned up his nose at the poor fellow, and ordered him to be off at once. Here are the lines:—

"As on the way I itinerated,
A rural person I obviated,
Interrogating time's transitation,
And of the passage demonstration.
My apprehension did ingenious scan
That he was merely a simplician;
So, when I saw he was extravagánt,
Unto the óbscure vulgar consonánt,
I bade him vanish most promiscuously,
And not contaminate my company."

39. Latin of the Fourth Period.— (iii) What happened in the case of the Norman-French contribution, happened also in this. The language became saturated with these new Latin words, until it became satiated, then, as it were, disgusted, and would take no more. Hundreds of

"Long-tailed words in osity and ation"

crowded into the English language; but many of them were doomed to speedy expulsion. Thus words like discerptibility, supervacaneousness, septentrionality, ludibundness (love of sport), came in in crowds. The verb intenerate tried to turn out soften; and deturpate to take the place of defile. But good writers, like Bacon and Raleigh, took care to avoid the use of such terms, and to employ only those Latin words which gave them the power to indicate a new idea— a new meaning or a new shade of meaning. And when we come to the eighteenth century, we find that a writer like Addison would have shuddered at the very mention of such "inkhorn terms."

40. Eye-Latin and Ear-Latin.— (i) One slight influence produced by this spread of devotion to classical Latin— to the Latin of Cicero and Livy, of Horace and Virgil— was to alter the spelling of French words. We had already received— through the ear— the French words assaute, aventure, defaut, dette, vitaille, and others. But when our scholars became accustomed to the book-form of these words in Latin books, they gradually altered them— for the eye and ear— into assault, adventure, default, debt, and victuals. They went further. A large number of Latin words that already existed in the language in their Norman-French form (for we must not forget that French is Latin "with the ends bitten off"— changed by being spoken peculiarly and heard imperfectly) were reintroduced in their original Latin form. Thus we had caitiff from the Normans; but we reintroduced it in the shape of captive, which comes almost unaltered from the Latin captivum. Feat we had from the Normans; but the Latin factum, which provided the word, presented us with a second form of it in the word fact. Such words might be called Ear-Latin and Eye-Latin; Mouth-Latin and Book-Latin; Spoken Latin and Written Latin; or Latin at second-hand and Latin at first-hand.

41. Eye-Latin and Ear-Latin.— (ii) This coming in of the same word by two different doors— by the Eye and by the Ear— has given rise to the phenomenon of Doublets. The following is a list of Latin Doublets; and it will be noticed that Latin1 stands for Latin at first-hand— from books; and Latin2 for Latin at second-hand— through the Norman-French.

LATIN DOUBLETS OR DUPLICATES.
LATIN.   LATIN1. LATIN2.

Antecessorem	Antecessor	Ancestor.
Benedictionem	Benediction	Benison.
Cadentia (Low Lat. noun)	Cadence	Chance.
Captivum	Captive	Caitiff.
Conceptionem	Conception	Conceit.
Consuetudinem	Consuetude	{Custom. {Costume.
Cophinum	Coffin	Coffer.
Corpus (a body)	Corpse	Corps.
Debitum (something owed)	Debit	Debt.
Defectum (something wanting)	Defect	Defeat.
Dilat[-a]re	Dilate	Delay.
Exemplum	Example	Sample.
Fabr[)i]ca (a workshop)	Fabric	Forge.
Factionem	Faction	Fashion.
Factum	Fact	Feat.
Fidelitatem	Fidelity	Fealty.
Fragilem	Fragile	Frail.
Gent[-i]lis (belonging to a gens or family)	Gentile	Gentle.
Historia	History	Story.
Hospitale	Hospital	Hotel.
Lectionem	Lection	Lesson.
Legalem	Legal	Loyal.
Magister	Master	Mr.
Majorem (greater)	Major	Mayor.
Maledictionem	Malediction	Malison.
Moneta	Mint	Money.
Nutrimentum	Nutriment	Nourishment.
Orationem	Oration	Orison (a prayer).
Paganum (a dweller in a pagus or country district)	Pagan	Payne (a proper name).
Particulam (a little part)	Particle	Parcel.
Pauperem	Pauper	Poor.
Penitentiam	Penitence	Penance.
Persecutum	Persecute	Pursue.
Potionem (a draught)	Potion	Poison.
Pungentem	Pungent	Poignant.
Quietum	Quiet	Coy.
Radius	Radius	Ray.
Reg[-a]lem	Regal	Royal.
Respectum	Respect	Respite.

Securum	Secure	Sure.
Seniorem	Senior	Sir.
Separatum	Separate	Sever.
Species	Species	Spice.
Statum	State	Estate.
Tractum	Tract	Trait.
Traditionem	Tradition	Treason.
Zelosum	Zealous	Jealous.

42. Remarks on the above Table. —The word benison, a blessing, may be contrasted with its opposite, malison, a curse. —Cadence is the falling of sounds; chance the befalling of events. —A caitiff was at first a captive— then a person who made no proper defence, but allowed himself to be taken captive. —A corps is a body of troops. —The word sample is found, in older English, in the form of ensample. —A feat of arms is a deed or fact of arms, par excellence. —To understand how fragile became frail, we must pronounce the g hard, and notice how the hard guttural falls easily away— as in our own native words flail and hail, which formerly contained a hard g. —A major is a greater captain; a mayor is a greater magistrate. —A magister means a bigger man— as opposed to a minister (from minus), a smaller man. —Moneta was the name given to a stamped coin, because these coins were first struck in the temple of Juno Moneta, Juno the Adviser or the Warner. (From the same root— mon— come monition, admonition; monitor; admonish.) —Shakespeare uses the word orison freely for prayer, as in the address of Hamlet to Ophelia, where he says, "Nymph, in thy orisons, be all my sins remembered!" —Poor comes to us from an Old French word poure; the newer French is pauvre. —To understand the vanishing of the g sound in poignant, we must remember that the Romans sounded it always hard. —Sever we get through separate, because p and v are both labials, and therefore easily interchangeable. —Treason— with its s instead of ti— may be compared with benison, malison, orison, poison, and reason.

43. Conclusions from the above Table.— If we examine the table on page 231 with care, we shall come to several undeniable conclusions. (i) First, the words which come to us direct from Latin are found more in books than in everyday speech. (ii) Secondly, they are longer. The reason is that the words that have come through French have been worn down by the careless pronunciation of many generations— by that desire for ease in the pronouncing of words which characterises all languages, and have at last been compelled to take that form which was least difficult to pronounce. (iii) Thirdly, the two sets of words have, in each case, either (a) very different meanings, or (b) different shades of meaning. There is no likeness of meaning in cadence and chance, except the common meaning of fall which belongs to the root from which they both spring. And the different shades of meaning between history and story, between regal and royal, between persecute and pursue, are also quite plainly marked, and are of the greatest use in composition.

44. Latin Triplets.— Still more remarkable is the fact that there are in our language words that have made three appearances— one through Latin, one through Norman-French, and one through ordinary French. These seem to live quietly side by side in the language; and no one asks by what claim they are here. They are useful: that is enough. These triplets are— regal, royal, and real; legal, loyal, and leal; fidelity, faithfulness,[8] and fealty. The adjective real we no longer possess in the sense of royal, but Chaucer uses it; and it still exists in the noun real-m. Leal is most used in Scotland, where it has a settled abode in the well-known phrase "the land o' the leal."

[8: The word faith is a true French word with an
English ending— the ending th. Hence it is a hybrid. The old
French word was fei— from the Latin fidem; and the ending
th was added to make it look more like truth, wealth,
health, and other purely English words.]

45. Greek Doublets.— The same double introduction, which we noticed in the case of Latin words, takes place in regard to Greek words. It seems to have been forgotten that our English forms of them had been already given us by St Augustine and the Church, and a newer form of each was reintroduced. The following are a few examples:—
GREEK. OLDER FORM. LATER FORM.

GREEK.	OLDER FORM.	LATER FORM.
Adamanta[9] (the untameable)	Diamond	Adamant.
Balsamon	Balm	Balsam.
Blasph[-e]mein (to speak ill of)	Blame	Blaspheme.
Cheirourgon[9] (a worker with the hand)	Chirurgeon	Surgeon.
Dact[)u]lon (a finger)	Date (the fruit)	Dactyl.
Phantasia	Fancy	Phantasy.
Phantasma (an appearance)	Phantom	Phantasm.
Presbuteron (an elder)	Priest	Presbyter.
Paralysis	Palsy	Paralysis.
Scand[)a]lon	Slander	Scandal.

[9: The accusative or objective case is given in all these words.]
It may be remarked of the word fancy, that, in Shakespeare's time, it meant love or imagination—
"Tell me, where is fancy bred,
Or in the heart, or in the head?"
It is now restricted to mean a lighter and less serious kind of imagination. Thus we say that Milton's 'Paradise Lost' is a work of imagination; but that Moore's 'Lalla Rookh' is a product of the poet's fancy.
46. Characteristics of the Two Elements of English.— If we keep our attention fixed on the two chief elements in our language— the English element

and the Latin element— the Teutonic and the Romance— we shall find some striking qualities manifest themselves. We have already said that whole sentences can be made containing only English words, while it is impossible to do this with Latin or other foreign words. Let us take two passages— one from a daily newspaper, and the other from Shakespeare:—

(i) "We find the functions of such an official defined in the
Act. He is to be a legally qualified medical practitioner
of skill and experience, to inspect and report periodically
on the sanitary condition of town or district; to ascertain
the existence of diseases, more especially epidemics
increasing the rates of mortality, and to point out the
existence of any nuisances or other local causes, which are
likely to originate and maintain such diseases, and
injuriously affect the health of the inhabitants of such town
or district; to take cognisance of the existence of any
contagious disease, and to point out the most efficacious
means for the ventilation of chapels, schools, registered
lodging-houses, and other public buildings."

In this passage, all the words in italics are either Latin or Greek. But, if the purely English words were left out, the sentence would fall into ruins— would become a mere rubbish-heap of words. It is the small particles that give life and motion to each sentence. They are the joints and hinges on which the whole sentence moves. —Let us now look at a passage from Shakespeare. It is from the speech of Macbeth, after he has made up his mind to murder Duncan:—

(ii) "Go bid thy mistress, when my drink is ready,
She strike upon the bell. Get thee to bed!—
Is this a dagger which I see before me,
The handle toward my hand? Come! let me clutch thee!
—I have thee not; and yet I see thee still."

In this passage there is only one Latin (or French) word— the word mistress. If Shakespeare had used the word lady, the passage would have been entirely English. —The passage from the newspaper deals with large generalisations; that from Shakespeare with individual acts and feelings— with things that come home "to the business and bosom" of man as man. Every master of the English language understands well the art of mingling the two elements— so as to obtain a fine effect; and none better than writers like Shakespeare, Milton, Gray, and Tennyson. Shakespeare makes Antony say of Cleopatra:—
"Age cannot wither her; nor custom stale
Her infinite variety."

Here the French (or Latin) words custom and variety form a vivid contrast to the English verb stale, throw up its meaning and colour, and give it greater prominence. —Milton makes Eve say:—

"I thither went
With inexperienc'd thought, and laid me down
On the green bank, to look into the clear
Smooth lake, that to me seem'd another sky."

Here the words inexperienced and clear give variety to the sameness of the English words. —Gray, in the Elegy, has this verse:—

"The breezy call of incense-breathing morn,
  The swallow twittering from the straw-built shed,
The cock's shrill clarion or the echoing horn,
  No more shall rouse them from their lowly bed."

Here incense, clarion, and echoing give a vivid colouring to the plainer hues of the homely English phrases. —Tennyson, in the Lotos-Eaters, vi., writes:—

"Dear is the memory of our wedded lives,
And dear the last embraces of our wives
And their warm tears: but all hath suffer'd change;
For surely now our household hearths are cold:
Our sons inherit us: our looks are strange:
And we should come like ghosts to trouble joy."

Most powerful is the introduction of the French words suffered change, inherit, strange, and trouble joy; for they give with painful force the contrast of the present state of desolation with the homely rest and happiness of the old abode, the love of the loving wives, the faithfulness of the stalwart sons.

47. English and other Doublets.— We have already seen how, by the presentation of the same word at two different doors— the door of Latin and the door of French— we are in possession of a considerable number of doublets. But this phenomenon is not limited to Latin and French— is not solely due to the contributions we receive from these languages. We find it also within English itself; and causes of the most different description bring about the same results. For various reasons, the English language is very rich in doublets. It possesses nearly five hundred pairs of such words. The language is all the richer for having them, as it is thereby enabled to give fuller and clearer expression to the different shades and delicate varieties of meaning in the mind.

48. The sources of doublets are various. But five different causes seem chiefly to have operated in producing them. They are due to differences of pronunciation; to differences in spelling; to contractions for convenience in daily speech; to differences in dialects; and to the fact that many of them come from

different languages. Let us look at a few examples of each. At bottom, however, all these differences will be found to resolve themselves into differences of pronunciation. They are either differences in the pronunciation of the same word by different tribes, or by men in different counties, who speak different dialects; or by men of different nations.

49. Differences in Pronunciation.— From this source we have parson and person (the parson being the person or representative of the Church); sop and soup; task and tax (the sk has here become ks); thread and thrid; ticket and etiquette; sauce and souse (to steep in brine); squall and squeal.

50. Differences in Spelling.— To and too are the same word— one being used as a preposition, the other as an adverb; of and off, from and fro, are only different spellings, which represent different functions or uses of the same word; onion and union are the same word. An union[10] comes from the Latin unus, one, and it meant a large single pearl— a unique jewel; the word was then applied to the plant, the head of which is of a pearl-shape.

[10: In Hamlet v. 2. 283, Shakespeare makes the King say—

"The King shall drink to Hamlet's better breath; And in the cup an union shall he throw."]

51. Contractions.— Contraction has been a pretty fruitful source of doublets in English. A long word has a syllable or two cut off; or two or three are compressed into one. Thus example has become sample; alone appears also as lone; amend has been shortened into mend; defend has been cut down into fend (as in fender); manoeuvre has been contracted into manure (both meaning originally to work with the hand); madam becomes 'm in yes 'm[11]; and presbyter has been squeezed down into priest.[12] Other examples of contraction are: capital and cattle; chirurgeon (a worker with the hand) and surgeon; cholera and choler (from ch()o]los, the Greek word for bile); disport and sport; estate and state; esquire and squire; Egyptian and gipsy; emmet and ant; gammon and game; grandfather and gaffer; grandmother and gammer; iota (the Greek letter i) and jot; maximum and maxim; mobile and mob; mosquito and musket; papa and pope; periwig and wig; poesy and posy; procurator and proctor; shallop and sloop; unity and unit. It is quite evident that the above pairs of words, although in reality one, have very different meanings and uses.

[11: Professor Max Müller gives this as the most
remarkable instance of cutting down. The Latin mea domina became
in French madame; in English ma'am; and, in the language of
servants, 'm.]

[12: Milton says, in one of his sonnets—
"New Presbyter is but old Priest writ large."
From the etymological point of view, the truth is just the other way about.
Priest is old Presbyter writ small.]

52. Difference of English Dialects.— Another source of doublets is to be found in the dialects of the English language. Almost every county in England

has its own dialect; but three main dialects stand out with great prominence in our older literature, and these are the Northern, the Midland, and the Southern. The grammar of these dialects[13] was different; their pronunciation of words was different— and this has given rise to a splitting of one word into two. In the North, we find a hard c, as in the caster of Lancaster; in the Midlands, a soft c, as in Leicester; in the South, a ch, as in Winchester. We shall find similar differences of hardness and softness in ordinary words. Thus we find kirk and church; canker and cancer; canal and channel; deck and thatch; drill and thrill; fan and van (in a winnowing-machine); fitch and vetch; hale and whole; mash and mess; naught, nought, and not; pike, peak, and beak; poke and pouch; quid (a piece of tobacco for chewing) and cud (which means the thing chewed); reave and rob; ridge and rig; scabby and shabby; scar and share; screech and shriek; shirt and skirt; shuffle and scuffle; spray and sprig; wain and waggon— and other pairs. All of these are but different modes of pronouncing the same word in different parts of England; but the genius of the language has taken advantage of these different ways of pronouncing to make different words out of them, and to give them different functions, meanings, and uses.

[13: See History of English Literature]

CHAPTER III.

HISTORY OF THE GRAMMAR OF ENGLISH.

1. The Oldest English Synthetic.— The oldest English, or Anglo-Saxon, that was brought over here in the fifth century, was a language that showed the relations of words to each other by adding different endings to words, or by synthesis. These endings are called inflexions. Latin and Greek are highly inflected languages; French and German have many more inflexions than modern English; and ancient English (or Anglo-Saxon) also possessed a large number of inflexions.

2. Modern English Analytic.— When, instead of inflexions, a language employs small particles— such as prepositions, auxiliary verbs, and suchlike words— to express the relations of words to each other, such a language is called analytic or non-inflexional. When we say, as we used to say in the oldest English, "God is ealra cyninga cyning," we speak a synthetic language. But when we say, "God is king of all kings," then we employ an analytic or uninflected language.

3. Short View of the History of English Grammar.— From the time when the English language came over to this island, it has grown steadily in the number of its words. On the other hand, it has lost just as steadily in the number of its inflexions. Put in a broad and somewhat rough fashion, it may be said that—

(i) Up to the year 1100— one generation after the Battle of Senlac— the English language was a SYNTHETIC Language.

(ii) From the year 1100 or thereabouts, English has been losing its inflexions, and gradually becoming more and more an ANALYTIC Language.

4. Causes of this Change.— Even before the coming of the Danes and the Normans, the English people had shown a tendency to get rid of some of their inflexions. A similar tendency can be observed at the present time among the Germans of the Rhine Province, who often drop an n at the end of a word, and show in other respects a carelessness about grammar. But, when a foreign people comes among natives, such a tendency is naturally encouraged, and often greatly increased. The natives discover that these inflexions are not so very important, if only they can get their meaning rightly conveyed to the foreigners. Both parties, accordingly, come to see that the root of the word is the most important element; they stick to that, and they come to neglect the mere inflexions. Moreover, the accent in English words always struck the root; and hence this part of the word always fell on the ear with the greater force, and carried the greater weight. When the Danes— who spoke a cognate language— began to settle in England, the tendency to drop inflexions increased; but when the Normans— who spoke an entirely different language— came, the tendency increased enormously, and the inflexions of Anglo-Saxon began to "fall as the

leaves fall" in the dry wind of a frosty October. Let us try to trace some of these changes and losses.

5. Grammar of the First Period, 450-1100.— The English of this period is called the Oldest English or Anglo-Saxon. The gender of nouns was arbitrary, or— it may be— poetical; it did not, as in modern English it does, follow the sex. Thus nama, a name, was masculine; tunge, a tongue, feminine; and eáge, an eye, neuter. Like nama, the proper names of men ended in a; and we find such names as Isa, Offa, Penda, as the names of kings. Nouns at this period had five cases, with inflexions for each; now we possess but one inflexion— that for the possessive. —Even the definite article was inflected. —The infinitive of verbs ended in an; and the sign to— which we received from the Danes— was not in use, except for the dative of the infinitive. This dative infinitive is still preserved in such phrases as "a house to let;" "bread to eat;" "water to drink." —The present participle ended in ende (in the North ande). This present participle may be said still to exist— in spoken, but not in written speech; for some people regularly say walkin, goin, for walking and going. —The plural of the present indicative ended in ath for all three persons. In the perfect tense, the plural ending was on. —There was no future tense; the work of the future was done by the present tense. Fragments of this usage still survive in the language, as when we say, "He goes up to town next week." —Prepositions governed various cases; and not always the objective (or accusative), as they do now.

6. Grammar of the Second Period, 1100-1250.— The English of this period is called Early English. Even before the coming of the Normans, the inflexions of our language had— as we have seen— begun to drop off, and it was slowly on the way to becoming an analytic language. The same changes— the same simplification of grammar, has taken place in nearly every Low German language. But the coming of the Normans hastened these changes, for it made the inflexional endings of words of much less practical importance to the English themselves. —Great changes took place in the pronunciation also. The hard c or k was softened into ch; and the hard guttural g was refined into a y or even into a silent w. —A remarkable addition was made to the language. The Oldest English or Anglo-Saxon had no indefinite article. They said ofer stán for on a rock. But, as the French have made the article un out of the Latin unus, so the English pared down the northern ane (= one) into the article an or a. The Anglo-Saxon definite article was se, seo, þaet; and in the grammar of this Second Period it became þe, þeo, þe. —The French plural in es took the place of the English plural in en. But housen and shoon existed for many centuries after the Norman coming; and Mr Barnes, the Dorsetshire poet, still deplores the ugly sound of nests and fists, and would like to be able to say and to write nesten and fisten. —The dative plural, which ended in um, becomes an e or an en. The um, however, still exists in the form of om in seldom (= at few times) and whilom (= in old times). —The gender of nouns falls into confusion, and begins to show a tendency to follow the sex. —Adjectives show a tendency to drop several of their inflexions, and to become as serviceable and accommodating as they are now— when they are the same with all numbers, genders, and cases. —The an

of the infinitive becomes en, and sometimes even the n is dropped. —Shall and will begin to be used as tense-auxiliaries for the future tense.

7. Grammar of the Third Period, 1250-1350.— The English of this period is often called Middle English. —The definite article still preserves a few inflexions. —Nouns that were once masculine or feminine become neuter, for the sake of convenience. —The possessive in es becomes general. —Adjectives make their plural in e. —The infinitive now takes to before it— except after a few verbs, like bid, see, hear, etc. —The present participle in inge makes its appearance about the year 1300.

8. Grammar of the Fourth Period, 1350-1485.— This may be called Later Middle English. An old writer of the fourteenth century points out that, in his time— and before it— the English language was "a-deled a thre," divided into three; that is, that there were three main dialects, the Northern, the Midland, and the Southern. There were many differences in the grammar of these dialects; but the chief of these differences is found in the plural of the present indicative of the verb. This part of the verb formed its plurals in the following manner:—

NORTHERN.	MIDLAND.	SOUTHERN.
We hopës	We hopen	We hopeth.
You hopës	You hopen	You hopeth.
They hopës	They hopen	They hopeth.[14]

In time the Midland dialect conquered; and the East Midland form of it became predominant all over England. As early as the beginning of the thirteenth century, this dialect had thrown off most of the old inflexions, and had become almost as flexionless as the English of the present day. Let us note a few of the more prominent changes. —The first personal pronoun Ic or Ich loses the guttural, and becomes I. —The pronouns him, them, and whom, which are true datives, are used either as datives or as objectives. —The imperative plural ends in eth. "Riseth up," Chaucer makes one of his characters say, "and stondeth by me!" —The useful and almost ubiquitous letter e comes in as a substitute for a, u, and even an. Thus nama becomes name, sunu (son) becomes sune, and withutan changes into withute. —The dative of adjectives is used as an adverb. Thus we find softë, brightë employed like our softly, brightly. —The n in the infinitive has fallen away; but the ë is sounded as a separate syllable. Thus we find brekë, smitë for breken and smiten.

[14: This plural we still find in the famous Winchester motto, "Manners maketh man."]

9. General View.— In the time of King Alfred, the West-Saxon speech— the Wessex dialect— took precedence of the rest, and became the literary dialect of England. But it had not, and could not have, any influence on the spoken language of other parts of England, for the simple reason that very few persons were able to travel, and it took days— and even weeks— for a man to go from Devonshire to Yorkshire. In course of time the Midland dialect— that spoken between the Humber and the Thames— became the predominant dialect of

England; and the East Midland variety of this dialect became the parent of modern standard English. This predominance was probably due to the fact that it, soonest of all, got rid of its inflexions, and became most easy, pleasant, and convenient to use. And this disuse of inflexions was itself probably due to the early Danish settlements in the east, to the larger number of Normans in that part of England, to the larger number of thriving towns, and to the greater and more active communication between the eastern seaports and the Continent. The inflexions were first confused, then weakened, then forgotten, finally lost. The result was an extreme simplification, which still benefits all learners of the English language. Instead of spending a great deal of time on the learning of a large number of inflexions, which are to them arbitrary and meaningless, foreigners have only to fix their attention on the words and phrases themselves, that is, on the very pith and marrow of the language— indeed, on the language itself. Hence the great German grammarian Grimm, and others, predict that English will spread itself all over the world, and become the universal language of the future. In addition to this almost complete sweeping away of all inflexions,— which made Dr Johnson say, "Sir, the English language has no grammar at all,"— there were other remarkable and useful results which accrued from the coming in of the Norman-French and other foreign elements.

10. Monosyllables.— The stripping off of the inflexions of our language cut a large number of words down to the root. Hundreds, if not thousands, of our verbs were dissyllables, but, by the gradual loss of the ending en (which was in Anglo-Saxon an), they became monosyllables. Thus bindan, drincan, findan, became bind, drink, find; and this happened with hosts of other verbs. Again, the expulsion of the guttural, which the Normans never could or would take to, had the effect of compressing many words of two syllables into one. Thus haegel, twaegen, and faegen, became hail, twain, and fain. —In these and other ways it has come to pass that the present English is to a very large extent of a monosyllabic character. So much is this the case, that whole books have been written for children in monosyllables. It must be confessed that the monosyllabic style is often dull, but it is always serious and homely. We can find in our translation of the Bible whole verses that are made up of words of only one syllable. Many of the most powerful passages in Shakespeare, too, are written in monosyllables. The same may be said of hundreds of our proverbs— such as, "Cats hide their claws"; "Fair words please fools"; "He that has most time has none to lose." Great poets, like Tennyson and Matthew Arnold, understand well the fine effect to be produced from the mingling of short and long words— of the homely English with the more ornate Romance language. In the following verse from Matthew Arnold the words are all monosyllables, with the exception of tired and contention (which is Latin):—

"Let the long contention cease;
Geese are swans, and swans are geese;
Let them have it how they will,
Thou art tired. Best be still!"

In Tennyson's "Lord of Burleigh," when the sorrowful husband comes to look upon his dead wife, the verse runs almost entirely in monosyllables:—

"And he came to look upon her,
  And he looked at her, and said:
'Bring the dress, and put it on her,
  That she wore when she was wed.'"

An American writer has well indicated the force of the English monosyllable in the following sonnet:—

"Think not that strength lies in the big, round word,
  Or that the brief and plain must needs be weak.
To whom can this be true who once has heard
  The cry for help, the tongue that all men speak,
When want, or fear, or woe, is in the throat,
  So that each word gasped out is like a shriek
Pressed from the sore heart, or a strange, wild note
  Sung by some fay or fiend! There is a strength,
Which dies if stretched too far, or spun too fine,
  Which has more height than breadth, more depth than length;
Let but this force of thought and speech be mine,
  And he that will may take the sleek fat phrase,
Which glows but burns not, though it beam and shine;
  Light, but no heat,— a flash, but not a blaze."

It will be observed that this sonnet consists entirely of monosyllables, and yet that the style of it shows considerable power and vigour. The words printed in italics are all derived from Latin, with the exception of the word phrase, which is Greek.

11. Change in the Order of Words.— The syntax— or order of words— of the oldest English was very different from that of Norman-French. The syntax of an Old English sentence was clumsy and involved; it kept the attention long on the strain; it was rumbling, rambling, and unpleasant to the ear. It kept the attention on the strain, because the verb in a subordinate clause was held back, and not revealed till we had come to the end of the clause. Thus the Anglo-Saxon wrote (though in different form and spelling)—

"When Darius saw, that he overcome be would."

The newer English, under French influence, wrote—

"When Darius saw that he was going to be overcome."

This change has made an English sentence lighter and more easy to understand, for the reader or hearer is not kept waiting for the verb; but each word comes just when it is expected, and therefore in its "natural" place. The Old English sentence— which is very like the German sentence of the present day— has been compared to a heavy cart without springs, while the newer English sentence is like a modern well-hung English carriage. Norman-French, then, gave us a brighter, lighter, freer rhythm, and therefore a sentence more easy to understand and to employ, more supple, and better adapted to everyday use.

12. The Expulsion of Gutturals.— (i) Not only did the Normans help us to an easier and pleasanter kind of sentence, they aided us in getting rid of the numerous throat-sounds that infested our language. It is a remarkable fact that there is not now in the French language a single guttural. There is not an h in the whole language. The French write an h in several of their words, but they never sound it. Its use is merely to serve as a fence between two vowels— to keep two vowels separate, as in la haine, hatred. No doubt the Normans could utter throat-sounds well enough when they dwelt in Scandinavia; but, after they had lived in France for several generations, they acquired a great dislike to all such sounds. No doubt, too, many, from long disuse, were unable to give utterance to a guttural. This dislike they communicated to the English; and hence, in the present day, there are many people— especially in the south of England— who cannot sound a guttural at all. The muscles in the throat that help to produce these sounds have become atrophied— have lost their power for want of practice. The purely English part of the population, for many centuries after the Norman invasion, could sound gutturals quite easily— just as the Scotch and the Germans do now; but it gradually became the fashion in England to leave them out.

13. The Expulsion of Gutturals.— (ii) In some cases the guttural disappeared entirely; in others, it was changed into or represented by other sounds. The ge at the beginning of the passive (or past) participles of many verbs disappeared entirely. Thus gebróht, gebóht, geworht, became brought, bought, and wrought. The g at the beginning of many words also dropped off. Thus Gyppenswich became Ipswich; gif became if; genoh, enough. —The guttural at the end of words— hard g or c— also disappeared. Thus halig became holy; eordhlic, earthly; gastlic, ghastly or ghostly. The same is the case in dough, through, plough, etc. —the guttural appearing to the eye but not to the ear. —Again, the guttural was changed into quite different sounds— into labials, into sibilants, into other sounds also. The following are a few examples:—

(a) The guttural has been softened, through Norman-French influence, into a sibilant. Thus rigg, egg, and brigg have become ridge, edge, and bridge.

(b) The guttural has become a labial— f— as in cough, enough, trough, laugh, draught, etc.

(c) The guttural has become an additional syllable, and is represented by a vowel-sound. Thus sorg and mearh have become sorrow and marrow.

(d) In some words it has disappeared both to eye and ear. Thus makëd has become made.

14. The Story of the GH.— How is it, then, that we have in so many words the two strongest gutturals in the language— g and h— not only separately, in so many of our words, but combined? The story is an odd one. Our Old English

or Saxon scribes wrote— not light, might, and night, but liht, miht, and niht. When, however, they found that the Norman-French gentlemen would not sound the h, and say— as is still said in Scotland— licht, &c., they redoubled the guttural, strengthened the h with a hard g, and again presented the dose to the Norman. But, if the Norman could not sound the h alone, still less could he sound the double guttural; and he very coolly let both alone— ignored both. The Saxon scribe doubled the signs for his guttural, just as a farmer might put up a strong wooden fence in front of a hedge; but the Norman cleared both with perfect ease and indifference. And so it came to pass that we have the symbol gh in more than seventy of our words, and that in most of these we do not sound it at all. The gh remains in our language, like a moss-grown boulder, brought down into the fertile valley in a glacial period, when gutturals were both spoken and written, and men believed in the truthfulness of letters— but now passed by in silence and noticed by no one.

15. The Letters that represent Gutturals.— The English guttural has been quite Protean in the written or printed forms it takes. It appears as an i, as a y, as a w, as a ch, as a dge, as a j, and— in its more native forms— as a g, a k, or a gh. The following words give all these forms: hail, day, fowl, teach, edge, ajar, drag, truck, and trough. Now hail was hagol, day was daeg, fowl was fugol, teach was taecan, edge was egg, ajar was achar. In seek, beseech, sought— which are all different forms of the same word— we see the guttural appearing in three different forms— as a hard k, as a soft ch, as an unnoticed gh. In think and thought, drink and draught, sly and sleight, dry and drought, slay and slaughter, it takes two different forms. In dig, ditch, and dike— which are all the same word in different shapes— it again takes three forms. In fly, flew, and flight, it appears as a y, a w, and a gh. But, indeed, the manners of a guttural, its ways of appearing and disappearing, are almost beyond counting.

16. Grammatical Result of the Loss of Inflexions.— When we look at a Latin or French or German word, we know whether it is a verb or a noun or a preposition by its mere appearance— by its face or by its dress, so to speak. But the loss of inflexions which has taken place in the English language has resulted in depriving us of this advantage— if advantage it is. Instead of looking at the face of a word in English, we are obliged to think of its function,— that is, of what it does. We have, for example, a large number of words that are both nouns and verbs— we may use them as the one or as the other; and, till we have used them, we cannot tell whether they are the one or the other. Thus, when we speak of "a cut on the finger," cut is a noun, because it is a name; but when we say, "Harry cut his finger," then cut is a verb, because it tells something about Harry. Words like bud, cane, cut, comb, cap, dust, fall, fish, heap, mind, name, pen, plaster, punt, run, rush, stone, and many others, can be used either as nouns or as verbs. Again, fast, quick, and hard may be used either as adverbs or as adjectives; and back may be employed as an adverb, as a noun, and even as an adjective. Shakespeare is very daring in the use of this licence. He makes one of his characters say, "But me no buts!" In this sentence, the first but is a verb in the imperative mood; the second is a noun in the objective case. Shakespeare

uses also such verbs as to glad, to mad, such phrases as a seldom pleasure, and the fairest she. Dr Abbott says, "In Elizabethan English, almost any part of speech can be used as any other part of speech. An adverb can be used as a verb, 'they askance their eyes'; as a noun, 'the backward and abysm of time'; or as an adjective, 'a seldom pleasure.' Any noun, adjective, or neuter verb can be used as an active verb. You can 'happy' your friend, 'malice' or 'fool' your enemy, or 'fall' an axe upon his neck." Even in modern English, almost any noun can be used as a verb. Thus we can say, "to paper a room"; "to water the horses"; "to black-ball a candidate"; to "iron a shirt" or "a prisoner"; "to toe the line." On the other hand, verbs may be used as nouns; for we can speak of a work, of a beautiful print, of a long walk, and so on.

46

CHAPTER IV.

SPECIMENS OF ENGLISH OF DIFFERENT PERIODS.

1. Vocabulary and Grammar.— The oldest English or Anglo-Saxon differs from modern English both in vocabulary and in grammar— in the words it uses and in the inflexions it employs. The difference is often startling. And yet, if we look closely at the words and their dress, we shall most often find that the words which look so strange are the very words with which we are most familiar— words that we are in the habit of using every day; and that it is their dress alone that is strange and antiquated. The effect is the same as if we were to dress a modern man in the clothes worn a thousand years ago: the chances are that we should not be able to recognise even our dearest friend.

2. A Specimen from Anglo-Saxon.— Let us take as an example a verse from the Anglo-Saxon version of one of the Gospels. The well-known verse, Luke ii. 40, runs thus in our oldest English version:—

Sóþlíce ðaet cild weox, and waes gestrangod, wisdómes full; and Godes gyfu waes on him.

Now this looks like an extract from a foreign language; but it is not: it is our own veritable mother-tongue. Every word is pure ordinary English; it is the dress— the spelling and the inflexions— that is quaint and old-fashioned. This will be plain from a literal translation:—

Soothly that child waxed, and was strengthened, wisdoms full (= full of wisdom); and God's gift was on him.

3. A Comparison.— This will become plainer if we compare the English of the Gospels as it was written in different periods of our language. The alteration in the meanings of words, the changes in the application of them, the variation in the use of phrases, the falling away of the inflexions— all these things become plain to the eye and to the mind as soon as we thoughtfully compare the different versions. The following are extracts from the Anglo-Saxon version (995), the version of Wycliffe (1389) and of Tyndale (1526), of the passage in Luke ii. 44, 45:—

ANGLO-SAXON.
WYCLIFFE.
TYNDALE.

Wéndon ðaet he on heora gefére wáere, ðá comon hig ánes daeges faer, and hine sóhton betweox his magas and his cúðan.

Forsothe thei gessinge him to be in the felowschipe, camen the wey of á day, and sou[gh]ten him among his cosyns and knowen.

For they supposed he had bene in the company, they cam a days iorney, and sought hym amonge their kynsfolke and acquayntaunce.

Ða hig hyne ne fúndon, hig gewendon to Hierusalem, hine sécende.

And thei not fyndinge, wenten a[gh]en to Jerusalem, sekynge him.

And founde hym not, they went backe agayne to Hierusalem, and sought hym.

The literal translation of the Anglo-Saxon version is as follows:—

(They) weened that he on their companionship were (= was), when came they one day's faring, and him sought betwixt his relations and his couth (folk = acquaintances).

When they him not found, they turned to Jerusalem, him seeking.

4. The Lord's Prayer.— The same plan of comparison may be applied to the different versions of the Lord's Prayer that have come down to us; and it will be seen from this comparison that the greatest changes have taken place in the grammar, and especially in that part of the grammar which contains the inflexions.

THE LORD'S PRAYER.

1130.
REIGN OF STEPHEN.
 1250.
REIGN OF HENRY III.
 1380.
WYCLIFFE'S VERSION.
 1526.
TYNDALE'S VERSION.

Fader ure, þe art on heofone.
Fadir ur, that es in hevene,
Our Fadir, that art in hevenys,
Our Father which art in heaven;

Sy gebletsod name þin,
Halud thi nam to nevene;
Halewid be thi name;
Halowed be thy name;

Cume þin rike.
Thou do as thi rich rike;
Thi kingdom come to;
Let thy kingdom come;

Si þin wil swa swa on heofone and on eorþan.
Thi will on erd be wrought, eek as it is wrought in heven ay.
Be thi wil done in erthe, as in hevene.
Thy will be fulfilled as well in earth as it is in heven.

Breod ure degwamlich geof us to daeg.
Ur ilk day brede give us to day.
Give to us this day oure breed ovir othir substaunce,
Geve us this day ur dayly bred,

And forgeof us ageltes ura swa swa we forgeofen agiltendum urum.
Forgive thou all us dettes urs, als we forgive till ur detturs.
And forgive to us our dettis, as we forgiven to oure
dettouris.
And forgeve us oure dettes as we forgeve ur detters.

And ne led us on costunge.
And ledde us in na fandung.
And lede us not into temptacioun;
And leade us not into temptation,

Ac alys us fram yfele. Swa beo hit.
But sculd us fra ivel thing. Amen.
But delyvere us from yvel. Amen.
But delyver us from evyll. For thyne is the kyngdom, and the
power, and the glorye, for ever. Amen.

It will be observed that Wycliffe's version contains five Romance terms—
substaunce, dettis, dettouris, temptacioun, and delyvere.

5. Oldest English and Early English.— The following is a short passage
from the Anglo-Saxon Chronicle, under date 1137: first, in the Anglo-Saxon
form; second, in Early English, or— as it has sometimes been called— Broken
Saxon; third, in modern English. The breaking-down of the grammar becomes
still more strikingly evident from this close juxtaposition.

(i) Hí swencton Þá wreccan menn
(ii) Hí swencten the wrecce men
(iii) They swinked (harassed) the wretched men

(i) Þaes landes mid castel-weorcum.
(ii) Of-the-land mid castel-weorces.
(iii) Of the land with castle-works.

(i) Ða Þá castelas waeron gemacod,
(ii) Tha the castles waren maked,
(iii) When the castles were made,

(i) Þá fyldon hí hí mid yfelum mannum.

(ii) thá fylden hi hi mid yvele men.

(iii) then filled they them with evil men.

6. Comparisons of Words and Inflexions.— Let us take a few of the most prominent words in our language, and observe the changes that have fallen upon them since they made their appearance in our island in the fifth century. These changes will be best seen by displaying them in columns:—

ANGLO-SAXON. EARLY ENGLISH. MIDDLE ENGLISH. MODERN ENGLISH.

ANGLO-SAXON.	EARLY ENGLISH.	MIDDLE ENGLISH.	MODERN ENGLISH.
heom.	to heom.	to hem.	to them.
seó.	heó.	ho, scho.	she.
sweostrum.	to the swestres.	to the swistren.	to the sisters.
geboren.	gebore.	iboré.	born.
lufigende.	lufigend.	lovand.	loving.
weoxon.	woxen.	wexide.	waxed.

7. Conclusions from the above Comparisons.— We can now draw several conclusions from the comparisons we have made of the passages given from different periods of the language. These conclusions relate chiefly to verbs and nouns; and they may become useful as a KEY to enable us to judge to what period in the history of our language a passage presented to us must belong. If we find such and such marks, the language is Anglo-Saxon; if other marks, it is Early English; and so on.

I.— MARKS OF ANGLO-SAXON.
II.— MARKS OF EARLY ENGLISH (1100-1250).
III.— MARKS OF MIDDLE ENGLISH (1250-1485).

VERBS.

Infinitive in an.
Infin. in en or e.
Infin. with to (the en was dropped about 1400).

Pres. part. in ende.
Pres. part. in ind.
Pres. part. in inge.

Past part. with ge.
ge of past part. turned into i or y.

3d plural pres. in ath.
3d plural past in on.

3d plural in en.
3d plural in en.

Plural of imperatives in ath.
Imperative in eth.
NOUNS.

Plurals in an, as, or a.
Plural in es.
Plurals in es (separate syllable).

Dative plural in um.
Dative plural in es.
Possessives in es (separate syllable).

8. The English of the Thirteenth Century.— In this century there was a great breaking-down and stripping-off of inflexions. This is seen in the Ormulum of Orm, a canon of the Order of St Augustine, whose English is nearly as flexionless as that of Chaucer, although about a century and a half before him. Orm has also the peculiarity of always doubling a consonant after a short vowel. Thus, in his introduction, he says:—

"Þiss boc iss nemmnedd Orrmulum
Forr þi þatt Orrm itt wrohhte."

That is, "This book is named Ormulum, for the (reason) that Orm wrought it." The absence of inflexions is probably due to the fact that the book is written in the East-Midland dialect. But, in a song called "The Story of Genesis and Exodus," written about 1250, we find a greater number of inflexions. Thus we read:—

"Hunger wex in lond Chanaan;
And his x sunes Jacob for-ðan
Sente in to Egypt to bringen coren;
He bilefe at hom ðe was gungest boren."

That is, "Hunger waxed (increased) in the land of Canaan; and Jacob for that (reason) sent his ten sons into Egypt to bring corn: he remained at home that was youngest born."

9. The English of the Fourteenth Century.— The four greatest writers of the fourteenth century are— in verse, Chaucer and Langlande; and in prose, Mandeville and Wycliffe. The inflexions continue to drop off; and, in Chaucer at least, a larger number of French words appear. Chaucer also writes in an elaborate verse-measure that forms a striking contrast to the homely rhythms of Langlande. Thus, in the "Man of Lawes Tale," we have the verse:—

"O queenës, lyvynge in prosperitée,
Duchessës, and ladyës everichone,
Haveth som routhe on hir adversitée;
An emperourës doughter stant allone;
She hath no wight to whom to make hir mone.
O blood roial! that stondest in this dredë
Fer ben thy frendës at thy gretë nedë!"

Here, with the exception of the imperative in Haveth som routhe (= have some pity), stant, and ben (= are), the grammar of Chaucer is very near the grammar of to-day. How different this is from the simple English of Langlande! He is speaking of the great storm of wind that blew on January 15, 1362:—

"Piries and Plomtres weore passchet to þe grounde,
In ensaumple to Men þat we scholde do þe bettre,
Beches and brode okes weore blowen to þe eorþe."

Here it is the spelling of Langlande's English that differs most from modern English, and not the grammar. —Much the same may be said of the style of Wycliffe (1324-1384) and of Mandeville (1300-1372). In Wycliffe's version of the Gospel of Mark, v. 26, he speaks of a woman "that hadde suffride many thingis of ful many lechis (doctors), and spendid alle hir thingis; and no-thing profitide." Sir John Mandeville's English keeps many old inflexions and spellings; but is, in other respects, modern enough. Speaking of Mahomet, he says: "And [gh]ee schulle understonds that Machamete was born in Arabye, that was first a pore knave that kept cameles, that wenten with marchantes for marchandise." Knave for boy, and wenten for went are the two chief differences— the one in the use of words, the other in grammar— that distinguish this piece of Mandeville's English from our modern speech.

10. The English of the Sixteenth Century.— This, which is also called Tudor-English, differs as regards grammar hardly at all from the English of the nineteenth century. This becomes plain from a passage from one of Latimer's sermons (1490-1555), "a book which gives a faithful picture of the manners, thoughts, and events of the period." "My father," he writes, "was a yeoman, and had no lands of his own, only he had a farm of three or four pound a year at the uttermost, and hereupon he tilled so much as kept half a dozen men. He had walk for a hundred sheep; and my mother milked thirty kine." In this passage, it is only the old-fashionedness, homeliness, and quaintness of the English— not its grammar— that makes us feel that it was not written in our own times. When Ridley, the fellow-martyr of Latimer, stood at the stake, he said, "I commit our cause to Almighty God, which shall indifferently judge all." Here he used indifferently in the sense of impartially— that is, in the sense of making no difference between parties; and this is one among a very large number of instances of Latin words, when they had not been long in our language, still retaining the older Latin meaning.

11. The English of the Bible (i).— The version of the Bible which we at present use was made in 1611; and we might therefore suppose that it is written in seventeenth-century English. But this is not the case. The translators were commanded by James I. to "follow the Bishops' Bible"; and the Bishops' Bible was itself founded on the "Great Bible," which was published in 1539. But the Great Bible is itself only a revision of Tyndale's, part of which appeared as early as 1526. When we are reading the Bible, therefore, we are reading English of the sixteenth century, and, to a large extent, of the early part of that century. It is true that successive generations of printers have, of their own accord, altered the spelling, and even, to a slight extent, modified the grammar. Thus we have fetched for the older fet, more for moe, sown for sowen, brittle for brickle (which gives the connection with break), jaws for chaws, sixth for sixt, and so on. But we still find such participles as shined and understanded; and such phrases as "they can skill to hew timber" (1 Kings v. 6), "abjects" for abject persons, "three days agone" for ago, the "captivated Hebrews" for "the captive Hebrews," and others.

12. The English of the Bible (ii).— We have, again, old words retained, or used in the older meaning. Thus we find, in Psalm v. 6, the phrase "them that speak leasing," which reminds us of King Alfred's expression about "leasum spellum" (lying stories). Trow and ween are often found; the "champaign over against Gilgal" (Deut. xi. 30) means the plain; and a publican in the New Testament is a tax-gatherer, who sent to the Roman Treasury or Publicum the taxes he had collected from the Jews. An "ill-favoured person" is an ill-looking person; and "bravery" (Isa. iii. 18) is used in the sense of finery in dress. —Some of the oldest grammar, too, remains, as in Esther viii. 8, "Write ye, as it liketh you," where the you is a dative. Again, in Ezek. xxx. 2, we find "Howl ye, Woe worth the day!" where the imperative worth governs day in the dative case. This idiom is still found in modern verse, as in the well-known lines in the first canto of the "Lady of the Lake":—
"Woe worth the chase, woe worth the day
That cost thy life, my gallant grey!"

CHAPTER V.

MODERN ENGLISH.

1. Grammar Fixed.— From the date of 1485— that is, from the beginning of the reign of Henry VII.— the changes in the grammar or constitution of our language are so extremely small, that they are hardly noticeable. Any Englishman of ordinary education can read a book belonging to the latter part of the fifteenth or to the sixteenth century without difficulty. Since that time the grammar of our language has hardly changed at all, though we have altered and enlarged our vocabulary, and have adopted thousands of new words. The introduction of Printing, the Revival of Learning, the Translation of the Bible, the growth and spread of the power to read and write— these and other influences tended to fix the language and to keep it as it is to-day. It is true that we have dropped a few old-fashioned endings, like the n or en in silvern and golden; but, so far as form or grammar is concerned, the English of the sixteenth and the English of the nineteenth centuries are substantially the same.

2. New Words.— But, while the grammar of English has remained the same, the vocabulary of English has been growing, and growing rapidly, not merely with each century, but with each generation. The discovery of the New World in 1492 gave an impetus to maritime enterprise in England, which it never lost, brought us into connection with the Spaniards, and hence contributed to our language several Spanish words. In the sixteenth and seventeenth centuries, Italian literature was largely read; Wyatt and Surrey show its influence in their poems; and Italian words began to come in in considerable numbers. Commerce, too, has done much for us in this way; and along with the article imported, we have in general introduced also the name it bore in its own native country. In later times, Science has been making rapid strides— has been bringing to light new discoveries and new inventions almost every week; and along with these new discoveries, the language has been enriched with new names and new terms. Let us look a little more closely at the character of these foreign contributions to the vocabulary of our tongue.

3. Spanish Words.— The words we have received from the Spanish language are not numerous, but they are important. In addition to the ill-fated word armada, we have the Spanish for Mr, which is Don (from Lat. dominus, a lord), with its feminine Duenna. They gave us also alligator, which is our English way of writing el lagarto, the lizard. They also presented us with a large number of words that end in o— such as buffalo, cargo, desperado, guano, indigo, mosquito, mulatto, negro, potato, tornado, and others. The following is a tolerably full list:—

Alligator.
Armada.
Barricade.
Battledore.
Bravado.
Buffalo.
Cargo.
Cigar.
Cochineal.
Cork.
Creole.
Desperado.
Don.
Duenna.
Eldorado.
Embargo.
Filibuster.
Flotilla.
Galleon (a ship).
Grandee.
Grenade.
Guerilla.
Indigo.
Jennet.
Matador.
Merino.
Mosquito.
Mulatto.
Negro.
Octoroon.
Quadroon.
Renegade.
Savannah.
Sherry (= Xeres).
Tornado.
Vanilla.

4. Italian Words.— Italian literature has been read and cultivated in England since the time of Chaucer— since the fourteenth century; and the arts and artists of Italy have for many centuries exerted a great deal of influence on those of England. Hence it is that we owe to the Italian language a large number of words. These relate to poetry, such as canto, sonnet, stanza; to music, as pianoforte, opera, oratorio, soprano, alto, contralto; to architecture and sculpture, as portico, piazza, cupola, torso; and to painting, as studio, fresco (an open-air painting), and others. The following is a complete list:—

Alarm.
Alert.
Alto.
Arcade.
Balcony.
Balustrade.
Bandit.
Bankrupt.
Bravo.
Brigade.
Brigand.
Broccoli.
Burlesque.
Bust.
Cameo.
Canteen.
Canto.
Caprice.
Caricature.
Carnival.
Cartoon.
Cascade.
Cavalcade.
Charlatan.
Citadel.
Colonnade.
Concert.
Contralto.
Conversazione.
Cornice.
Corridor.
Cupola.
Curvet.
Dilettante.
Ditto.
Doge.
Domino.
Extravaganza.
Fiasco.
Folio.
Fresco.
Gazette.
Gondola.
Granite.

Grotto.
Guitar.
Incognito.
Influenza.
Lagoon.
Lava.
Lazaretto.
Macaroni.
Madonna.
Madrigal.
Malaria.
Manifesto.
Motto.
Moustache.
Niche.
Opera.
Oratorio.
Palette.
Pantaloon.
Parapet.
Pedant.
Pianoforte.
Piazza.
Pistol.
Portico.
Proviso.
Quarto.
Regatta.
Ruffian.
Serenade.
Sonnet.
Soprano.
Stanza.
Stiletto.
Stucco.
Studio.
Tenor.
Terra-cotta.
Tirade.
Torso.
Trombone.
Umbrella.
Vermilion.
Vertu.
Virtuoso.

Vista.
Volcano.
Zany.

5. Dutch Words.— We have had for many centuries commercial dealings with the Dutch; and as they, like ourselves, are a great seafaring people, they have given us a number of words relating to the management of ships. In the fourteenth century, the southern part of the German Ocean was the most frequented sea in the world; and the chances of plunder were so great that ships of war had to keep cruising up and down to protect the trading vessels that sailed between England and the Low Countries. The following are the words which we owe to the Netherlands:—

Ballast.
Boom.
Boor.
Burgomaster.
Hoy.
Luff.
Reef.
Schiedam (gin).
Skates.
Skipper.
Sloop.
Smack.
Smuggle.
Stiver.
Taffrail.
Trigger.
Wear (said of a ship).
Yacht.
Yawl.

6. French Words.— Besides the large additions to our language made by the Norman-French, we have from time to time imported direct from France a number of French words, without change in the spelling, and with little change in the pronunciation. The French have been for centuries the most polished nation in Europe; from France the changing fashions in dress spread over all the countries of the Continent; French literature has been much read in England since the time of Charles II.; and for a long time all diplomatic correspondence between foreign countries and England was carried on in French. Words relating to manners and customs are common, such as soirée, etiquette, séance, élite; and we have also the names of things which were invented in France, such as mitrailleuse, carte-de-visite, coup d'état, and others. Some of these words are, in

spelling, exactly like English; and advantage of this has been taken in a well-known epigram:—

The French have taste in all they do,
  Which we are quite without;
For Nature, which to them gave goût,[15]
  To us gave only gout.

  The following is a list of French words which have been imported in comparatively recent times:—

Aide-de-camp.
Belle.
Bivouac.
Blonde.
Bouquet.
Brochure.
Brunette.
Brusque.
Carte-de-visite.
Coup-d'état.
Débris.
Début.
Déjeûner.
Depot.
Éclat.
Ennui.
Etiquette.
Façade.
Goût.
Naïve.
Naïveté.
Nonchalance.
Outré.
Penchant.
Personnel.
Précis.
Programme.
Protégé.
Recherché.
Séance.
Soirée.
Trousseau.

The Scotch have always had a closer connection with the French nation than England; and hence we find in the Scottish dialect of English a number of French words that are not used in South Britain at all. A leg of mutton is called in Scotland a gigot; the dish on which it is laid is an asher (from assiette); a cup for tea or for wine is a tassie (from tasse); the gate of a town is called the port; and a stubborn person is dour (Fr. dur, from Lat. durus); while a gentle and amiable person is douce (Fr. douce, Lat. dulcis).

[15: Goût (goo) from Latin gustus, taste.]

7. German Words.— It must not be forgotten that English is a Low-German dialect, while the German of books is New High-German. We have never borrowed directly from High-German, because we have never needed to borrow. Those modern German words that have come into our language in recent times are chiefly the names of minerals, with a few striking exceptions, such as loafer, which came to us from the German immigrants to the United States, and plunder, which seems to have been brought from Germany by English soldiers who had served under Gustavus Adolphus. The following are the German words which we have received in recent times:—

Cobalt.
Felspar.
Hornblende.
Landgrave.
Loafer.
Margrave.
Meerschaum.
Nickel.
Plunder.
Poodle.
Quartz.
Zinc.

8. Hebrew Words.— These, with very few exceptions, have come to us from the translation of the Bible, which is now in use in our homes and churches. Abbot and abbey come from the Hebrew word abba, father; and such words as cabal and Talmud, though not found in the Old Testament, have been contributed by Jewish literature. The following is a tolerably complete list:—

Abbey.
Abbot.
Amen.
Behemoth.
Cabal.
Cherub.
Cinnamon.
Hallelujah.

Hosannah.
Jehovah.
Jubilee.
Gehenna.
Leviathan.
Manna.
Paschal.
Pharisee.
Pharisaical.
Rabbi.
Sabbath.
Sadducees.
Satan.
Seraph.
Shibboleth.
Talmud.

9. Other Foreign Words.— The English have always been the greatest travellers in the world; and our sailors always the most daring, intelligent, and enterprising. There is hardly a port or a country in the world into which an English ship has not penetrated; and our commerce has now been maintained for centuries with every people on the face of the globe. We exchange goods with almost every nation and tribe under the sun. When we import articles or produce from abroad, we in general import the native name along with the thing. Hence it is that we have guano, maize, and tomato from the two Americas; coffee, cotton, and tamarind from Arabia; tea, congou, and nankeen from China; calico, chintz, and rupee from Hindostan; bamboo, gamboge, and sago from the Malay Peninsula; lemon, musk, and orange from Persia; boomerang and kangaroo from Australia; chibouk, ottoman, and tulip from Turkey. The following are lists of these foreign words; and they are worth examining with the greatest minuteness:—
AFRICAN DIALECTS.

Baobab.
Canary.
Chimpanzee.
Gnu.
Gorilla.
Guinea.
Karoo.
Kraal.
Oasis.
Quagga.
Zebra.

AMERICAN TONGUES.

Alpaca.
Buccaneer.
Cacique.
Cannibal.
Canoe.
Caoutchouc.
Cayman.
Chocolate.
Condor.
Guano.
Hammock.
Jaguar.
Jalap.
Jerked (beef).
Llama.
Mahogany.
Maize.
Manioc.
Moccasin.
Mustang.
Opossum.
Pampas.
Pemmican.
Potato.
Racoon.
Skunk.
Squaw.
Tapioca.
Tobacco.
Tomahawk.
Tomato.
Wigwam.

ARABIC.
(The word al means the. Thus alcohol = the spirit.)

Admiral (Milton writes ammiral).
Alcohol.
Alcove.
Alembic.
Algebra.
Alkali.
Amber.

Arrack.
Arsenal.
Artichoke.
Assassin.
Assegai.
Attar.
Azimuth.
Azure.
Caliph.
Carat.
Chemistry.
Cipher.
Civet.
Coffee.
Cotton.
Crimson.
Dragoman.
Elixir.
Emir.
Fakir.
Felucca.
Gazelle.
Giraffe.
Harem.
Hookah.
Koran (or Alcoran).
Lute.
Magazine.
Mattress.
Minaret.
Mohair.
Monsoon.
Mosque.
Mufti.
Nabob.
Nadir.
Naphtha.
Saffron.
Salaam.
Senna.
Sherbet.
Shrub (the drink).
Simoom.
Sirocco.
Sofa.

Sultan.
Syrup.
Talisman.
Tamarind.
Tariff.
Vizier.
Zenith.
Zero.

CHINESE.

Bohea.
China.
Congou.
Hyson.
Joss.
Junk.
Nankeen.
Pekoe.
Silk.
Souchong.
Tea.
Typhoon.

HINDU.

Avatar.
Banyan.
Brahmin.
Bungalow.
Calico.
Chintz.
Coolie.
Cowrie.
Durbar.
Jungle.
Lac (of rupees).
Loot.
Mulligatawny.
Musk.
Pagoda.
Palanquin.
Pariah.
Punch.
Pundit.

64

Rajah.
Rupee.
Ryot.
Sepoy.
Shampoo.
Sugar.
Suttee.
Thug.
Toddy.

HUNGARIAN.

Hussar.
Sabre.
Shako.
Tokay.

MALAY.

Amuck.
Bamboo.
Bantam.
Caddy.
Cassowary.
Cockatoo.
Dugong.
Gamboge.
Gong.
Gutta-percha.
Mandarin.
Mango.
Orang-outang.
Rattan.
Sago.
Upas.

PERSIAN.

Awning.
Bazaar.
Bashaw.
Caravan.
Check.
Checkmate.
Chess.

Curry.
Dervish.
Divan.
Firman.
Hazard.
Horde.
Houri.
Jar.
Jackal.
Jasmine.
Lac (a gum).
Lemon.
Lilac.
Lime (the fruit).
Musk.
Orange.
Paradise.
Pasha.
Rook.
Saraband.
Sash.
Scimitar.
Shawl.
Taffeta.
Turban.

POLYNESIAN DIALECTS.

Boomerang.
Kangaroo.
Taboo.
Tattoo.

PORTUGUESE.

Albatross.
Caste.
Cobra.
Cocoa-nut.
Commodore.
Fetish.
Lasso.
Marmalade.
Moidore.
Molasses.

Palaver.
Port (= Oporto).

RUSSIAN.

Czar.
Drosky.
Knout.
Morse.
Rouble.
Steppe.
Ukase.
Verst.

TARTAR.
Khan.
TURKISH.

Bey.
Caftan.
Chibouk.
Chouse.
Dey.
Janissary.
Kiosk.
Odalisque.
Ottoman.
Tulip.
Yashmak.
Yataghan.

10. Scientific Terms.— A very large number of discoveries in science have been made in this century; and a large number of inventions have introduced these discoveries to the people, and made them useful in daily life. Thus we have telegraph and telegram; photograph; telephone and even photophone. The word dynamite is also modern; and the unhappy employment of it has made it too widely known. Then passing fashions have given us such words as athlete and æsthete. In general, it may be said that, when we wish to give a name to a new thing— a new discovery, invention, or fashion— we have recourse not to our own stores of English, but to the vocabularies of the Latin and Greek languages.

LANDMARKS IN THE HISTORY OF THE ENGLISH LANGUAGE.

450
1. The Beowulf, an old English epic, "written on the mainland"
597
2. Christianity introduced by St Augustine (and with it many Latin and a few Greek words)
670
3. Caedmon— 'Paraphrase of the Scriptures,'— first English poem
735
4. Baeda— "The Venerable Bede"— translated into English part of St John's Gospel

901
5. King Alfred translated several Latin works into English, among others, Bede's 'Ecclesiastical History of the English Nation' (851)

1000
6. Aelfric, Archbishop of York, turned into English most of the historical books of the Old Testament

1066
7. The Norman Conquest, which introduced Norman French words

1160
8. Anglo-Saxon Chronicle, said to have been begun by King Alfred, and brought to a close in [1160]

1200
9. Orm or Orrmin's Ormulum, a poem written in the East Midland dialect, about [1200]

1204
10. Normandy lost under King John. Norman-English now have their only home in England, and use our English speech more and more

1205
11. Layamon translates the 'Brut' from the French of Robert Wace. This is the first English book (written in Southern English) after the stoppage of the Anglo-Saxon Chronicle

1220
12. The Ancren Riwle ("Rules for Anchorites") written in the Dorsetshire dialect. "It is the forerunner of a wondrous change in

our speech." "It swarms with French words"

1258
13. First Royal Proclamation in English, issued by Henry III.

1300
14. Robert of Gloucester's Chronicle (swarms with foreign terms)

1303
15. Robert Manning, "Robert of Brunn," compiles the 'Handlyng Synne.' "It contains a most copious proportion of French words"

1340
16. Ayenbite of Inwit (= "Remorse of Conscience")

1349
17. The Great Plague. After this it becomes less and less the fashion to speak French

1356
18. Sir John Mandeville, first writer of the newer English Prose— in his 'Travels,' which contained a large admixture of French words. "His English is the speech spoken at Court in the latter days of King Edward III."

1362
19. English becomes the language of the Law Courts

1380
20. Wickliffe's Bible

1400
21. Geoffrey Chaucer, the first great English poet, author of the 'Canterbury Tales'; born in 1340, died [1400]

1471
22. William Caxton, the first English printer, brings out (in the Low Countries) the first English book ever printed, the 'Recuyell of the Historyes of Troye,'— "not written with pen and ink, as other books are, to the end that every man may have them at once"

1474
23. First English Book printed in England (by Caxton) the 'Game and Playe of the Chesse'
1523

24. Lord Berners' translation of Froissart's Chronicle

1526-30
25. William Tyndale, by his translation of the Bible "fixed our
tongue once for all." "His New Testament has become the standard of
our tongue: the first ten verses of the Fourth Gospel are a good
sample of his manly Teutonic pith"

1590
26. Edmund Spenser publishes his 'Faerie Queene.' "Now began the
golden age of England's literature; and this age was to last for
about fourscore years"

1611
27. Our English Bible, based chiefly on Tyndale's translation.
"Those who revised the English Bible in 1611 were bidden to keep as
near as they could to the old versions, such as Tyndale's"

1616
28. William Shakespeare carried the use of the English language
to the greatest height of which it was capable. He employed 15,000
words. "The last act of 'Othello' is a rare specimen of
Shakespeare's diction: of every five nouns, verbs, and adverbs, four
are Teutonic"   (Born 1564)

1667
29. John Milton, "the most learned of English poets," publishes
his 'Paradise Lost,'— "a poem in which Latin words are introduced
with great skill"

1661
30. The Prayer-Book revised and issued in its final form. "Are
was substituted for be in forty-three places. This was a great
victory of the North over the South"

1688
31. John Bunyan writes his 'Pilgrim's Progress'— a book full of
pithy English idiom. "The common folk had the wit at once to see the
worth of Bunyan's masterpiece, and the learned long afterwards
followed in the wake of the common folk"   (Born 1628)

1642
32. Sir Thomas Browne, the author of 'Urn-Burial' and other works
written in a highly Latinised diction, such as the 'Religio Medici,'
written [1642]

1759

33. Dr Samuel Johnson was the chief supporter of the use of "long-tailed words in osity and ation," such as his novel called 'Rasselas,' published [1759]

34. Tennyson, Poet-Laureate, a writer of the best English— "a countryman of Robert Manning's, and a careful student of old Malory, has done much for the revival of pure English among us" (Born 1809)

PART IV.

OUTLINE OF THE HISTORY OF ENGLISH LITERATURE

CHAPTER I.

OUR OLDEST ENGLISH LITERATURE.

1. Literature.— The history of English Literature is, in its external aspect, an account of the best books in prose and in verse that have been written by English men and English women; and this account begins with a poem brought over from the Continent by our countrymen in the fifth century, and comes down to the time in which we live. It covers, therefore, a period of nearly fourteen hundred years.

2. The Distribution of Literature.— We must not suppose that literature has always existed in the form of printed books. Literature is a living thing— a living outcome of the living mind; and there are many ways in which it has been distributed to other human beings. The oldest way is, of course, by one person repeating a poem or other literary composition he has made to another; and thus literature is stored away, not upon book-shelves, but in the memory of living men. Homer's poems are said to have been preserved in this way to the Greeks for five hundred years. Father chanted them to son; the sons to their sons; and so on from generation to generation. The next way of distributing literature is by the aid of signs called letters made upon leaves, flattened reeds, parchment, or the inner bark of trees. The next is by the help of writing upon paper. The last is by the aid of type upon paper. This has existed in England for more than four hundred years— since the year 1474; and thus it is that our libraries contain many hundreds of thousands of valuable books. For the same reason is it, most probably, that as our power of retaining the substance and multiplying the copies of books has grown stronger, our living memories have grown weaker. This defect can be remedied only by education— that is, by training the memories of the young. While we possess so many printed books, it must not be forgotten that many valuable works exist still in manuscript— written either upon paper or on parchment.

3. Verse, the earliest form of Literature.— It is a remarkable fact that the earliest kind of composition in all languages is in the form of Verse. The oldest books, too, are those which are written in verse. Thus Homer's poems are the oldest literary work of Greece; the Sagas are the oldest productions of Scandinavian literature; and the Beowulf is the oldest piece of literature produced by the Anglo-Saxon race. It is also from the strong creative power and the lively inventions of poets that we are even now supplied with new thoughts and new language— that the most vivid words and phrases come into the language; just as it is the ranges of high mountains that send down to the plains the ever fresh soil that gives to them their unending fertility. And thus it happens that our present English speech is full of words and phrases that have found their way into the most ordinary conversation from the writings of our

great poets— and especially from the writings of our greatest poet, Shakespeare. The fact that the life of prose depends for its supplies on the creative minds of poets has been well expressed by an American writer:—

"I looked upon a plain of green,
  Which some one called the Land of Prose,
Where many living things were seen
  In movement or repose.

I looked upon a stately hill
  That well was named the Mount of Song,
Where golden shadows dwelt at will,
  The woods and streams among.

But most this fact my wonder bred
  (Though known by all the nobly wise),
It was the mountain stream that fed
  That fair green plain's amenities."

4. Our oldest English Poetry.— The verse written by our old English writers was very different in form from the verse that appears now from the hands of Tennyson, or Browning, or Matthew Arnold. The old English or Anglo-Saxon writers used a kind of rhyme called head-rhyme or alliteration; while, from the fourteenth century downwards, our poets have always employed end-rhyme in their verses.
  "{L}ightly down {l}eaping he {l}oosened his helmet."
Such was the rough old English form. At least three words in each long line were alliterative— two in the first half, and one in the second. Metaphorical phrases were common, such as war-adder for arrow, war-shirts for armour, whale's-path or swan-road for the sea, wave-horse for a ship, tree-wright for carpenter. Different statements of the same fact, different phrases for the same thing— what are called parallelisms in Hebrew poetry— as in the line—
  "Then saw they the sea head-lands— the windy walls,"
were also in common use among our oldest English poets.
  5. Beowulf.— The Beowulf is the oldest poem in the English language. It is our "old English epic"; and, like much of our ancient verse, it is a war poem. The author of it is unknown. It was probably composed in the fifth century— not in England, but on the Continent— and brought over to this island— not on paper or on parchment— but in the memories of the old Jutish or Saxon vikings or warriors. It was not written down at all, even in England, till the end of the ninth century, and then, probably, by a monk of Northumbria. It tells among other things the story of how Beowulf sailed from Sweden to the help of Hrothgar, a king in Jutland, whose life was made miserable by a monster— half man, half fiend— named Grendel. For about twelve years this monster had been in the habit of creeping up to the banqueting-hall of King Hrothgar, seizing

upon his thanes, carrying them off, and devouring them. Beowulf attacks and overcomes the dragon, which is mortally wounded, and flees away to die. The poem belongs both to the German and to the English literature; for it is written in a Continental English, which is somewhat different from the English of our own island. But its literary shape is, as has been said, due to a Christian writer of Northumbria; and therefore its written or printed form— as it exists at present— is not German, but English. Parts of this poem were often chanted at the feasts of warriors, where all sang in turn as they sat after dinner over their cups of mead round the massive oaken table. The poem consists of 3184 lines, the rhymes of which are solely alliterative.

6. The First Native English Poem.— The Beowulf came to us from the Continent; the first native English poem was produced in Yorkshire. On the dark wind-swept cliff which rises above the little land-locked harbour of Whitby, stand the ruins of an ancient and once famous abbey. The head of this religious house was the Abbess Hild or Hilda: and there was a secular priest in it,— a very shy retiring man, who looked after the cattle of the monks, and whose name was Caedmon. To this man came the gift of song, but somewhat late in life. And it came in this wise. One night, after a feast, singing began, and each of those seated at the table was to sing in his turn. Caedmon was very nervous— felt he could not sing. Fear overcame his heart, and he stole quietly away from the table before the turn could come to him. He crept off to the cowshed, lay down on the straw and fell asleep. He dreamed a dream; and, in his dream, there came to him a voice: "Caedmon, sing me a song!" But Caedmon answered: "I cannot sing; it was for this cause that I had to leave the feast." "But you must and shall sing!" "What must I sing, then?" he replied. "Sing the beginning of created things!" said the vision; and forthwith Caedmon sang some lines in his sleep, about God and the creation of the world. When he awoke, he remembered some of the lines that had come to him in sleep, and, being brought before Hilda, he recited them to her. The Abbess thought that this wonderful gift, which had come to him so suddenly, must have come from God, received him into the monastery, made him a monk, and had him taught sacred history. "All this Caedmon, by remembering, and, like a clean animal, ruminating, turned into sweetest verse." His poetical works consist of a metrical paraphrase of the Old and the New Testament. It was written about the year 670; and he died in 680. It was read and re-read in manuscript for many centuries, but it was not printed in a book until the year 1655.

7. The War-Poetry of England.— There were many poems about battles, written both in Northumbria and in the south of England; but it was only in the south that these war-songs were committed to writing; and of these written songs there are only two that survive up to the present day. These are the Song of Brunanburg, and the Song of the Fight at Maldon. The first belongs to the date 938; the second to 991. The Song of Brunanburg was inscribed in the SAXON CHRONICLE— a current narrative of events, written chiefly by monks, from the ninth century to the end of the reign of Stephen. The song tells the story of the fight of King Athelstan with Anlaf the Dane. It tells how five

young kings and seven earls of Anlaf's host fell on the field of battle, and lay there "quieted by swords," while their fellow-Northmen fled, and left their friends and comrades to "the screamers of war— the black raven, the eagle, the greedy battle-hawk, and the grey wolf in the wood." The Song of the Fight at Maldon tells us of the heroic deeds and death of Byrhtnoth, an ealdorman of Northumbria, in battle against the Danes at Maldon, in Essex. The speeches of the chiefs are given; the single combats between heroes described; and, as in Homer, the names and genealogies of the foremost men are brought into the verse.

8. The First English Prose.— The first writer of English prose was Baeda, or, as he is generally called, the Venerable Bede. He was born in the year 672 at Monkwearmouth, a small town at the mouth of the river Wear, and was, like Caedmon, a native of the kingdom of Northumbria. He spent most of his life at the famous monastery of Jarrow-on-Tyne. He spent his life in writing. His works, which were written in Latin, rose to the number of forty-five; his chief work being an Ecclesiastical History. But though Latin was the tongue in which he wrote his books, he wrote one book in English; and he may therefore be fairly considered the first writer of English prose. This book was a Translation of the Gospel of St John— a work which he laboured at until the very moment of his death. His disciple Cuthbert tells the story of his last hours. "Write quickly!" said Baeda to his scribe, for he felt that his end could not be far off. When the last day came, all his scholars stood around his bed. "There is still one chapter wanting, Master," said the scribe; "it is hard for thee to think and to speak." "It must be done," said Baeda; "take thy pen and write quickly." So through the long day they wrote— scribe succeeding scribe; and when the shades of evening were coming on, the young writer looked up from his task and said, "There is yet one sentence to write, dear Master." "Write it quickly!" Presently the writer, looking up with joy, said, "It is finished!" "Thou sayest truth," replied the weary old man; "it is finished: all is finished." Quietly he sank back upon his pillow, and, with a psalm of praise upon his lips, gently yielded up to God his latest breath. It is a great pity that this translation— the first piece of prose in our language— is utterly lost. No MS. of it is at present known to be in existence.

9. The Father of English Prose.— For several centuries, up to the year 866, the valleys and shores of Northumbria were the homes of learning and literature. But a change was not long in coming. Horde after horde of Danes swept down upon the coasts, ravaged the monasteries, burnt the books— after stripping the beautiful bindings of the gold, silver, and precious stones which decorated them— killed or drove away the monks, and made life, property, and thought insecure all along that once peaceful and industrious coast. Literature, then, was forced to desert the monasteries of Northumbria, and to seek for a home in the south— in Wessex, the kingdom over which Alfred the Great reigned for more than thirty years. The capital of Wessex was Winchester; and an able writer says: "As Whitby is the cradle of English poetry, so is Winchester of English prose." King Alfred founded colleges, invited to England men of learning from abroad,

and presided over a school for the sons of his nobles in his own Court. He himself wrote many books, or rather, he translated the most famous Latin books of his time into English. He translated into the English of Wessex, for example, the 'Ecclesiastical History' of Baeda; the 'History of Orosius,' into which he inserted geographical chapters of his own; and the 'Consolations of Philosophy,' by the famous Roman writer, Boëthius. In these books he gave to his people, in their own tongue, the best existing works on history, geography, and philosophy.

10. The Anglo-Saxon Chronicle.— The greatest prose-work of the oldest English, or purely Saxon, literature, is a work— not by one person, but by several authors. It is the historical work which is known as The Saxon Chronicle. It seems to have been begun about the middle of the ninth century; and it was continued, with breaks now and then, down to 1154— the year of the death of Stephen and the accession of Henry II. It was written by a series of successive writers, all of whom were monks; but Alfred himself is said to have contributed to it a narrative of his own wars with the Danes. The Chronicle is found in seven separate forms, each named after the monastery in which it was written. It was the newspaper, the annals, and the history of the nation. "It is the first history of any Teutonic people in their own language; it is the earliest and most venerable monument of English prose." This Chronicle possesses for us a twofold value. It is a valuable storehouse of historical facts; and it is also a storehouse of specimens of the different states of the English language— as regards both words and grammar— from the eighth down to the twelfth century.

11. Layamon's Brut.— Layamon was a native of Worcestershire, and a priest of Ernley on the Severn. He translated, about the year 1205, a poem called Brut, from the French of a monkish writer named Master Wace. Wace's work itself is little more than a translation of parts of a famous "Chronicle or History of the Britons," written in Latin by Geoffrey of Monmouth, who was Bishop of St Asaph in 1152. But Geoffrey himself professed only to have translated from a chronicle in the British or Celtic tongue, called the "Chronicle of the Kings of Britain," which was found in Brittany— long the home of most of the stories, traditions, and fables about the old British Kings and their great deeds. Layamon's poem called the "Brut" is a metrical chronicle of Britain from the landing of Brutus to the death of King Cadwallader, about the end of the seventh century. Brutus was supposed to be a great-grandson of Æneas, who sailed west and west till he came to Great Britain, where he settled with his followers. —This metrical chronicle is written in the dialect of the West of England; and it shows everywhere a breaking down of the grammatical forms of the oldest English, as we find it in the Anglo-Saxon Chronicle. In fact, between the landing of the Normans and the fourteenth century, two things may be noted: first, that during this time— that is, for three centuries— the inflections of the oldest English are gradually and surely stripped off; and, secondly, that there is little or no original English literature given to the country, but that by far the greater part consists chiefly of translations from French or from Latin.

12. Orm's Ormulum.— Less than half a century after Layamon's Brut appeared a poem called the Ormulum, by a monk of the name of Orm or Ormin. It was probably written about the year 1215. Orm was a monk of the order of St Augustine, and his book consists of a series of religious poems. It is the oldest, purest, and most valuable specimen of thirteenth-century English, and it is also remarkable for its peculiar spelling. It is written in the purest English, and not five French words are to be found in the whole poem of twenty thousand short lines. Orm, in his spelling, doubles every consonant that has a short vowel before it; and he writes pann for pan, but pan for pane. The following is a specimen of his poem:—

Ice hafe wennd inntill Ennglissh
Goddspelless hallghe lare,
Affterr thatt little witt tatt me
Min Drihhtin hafethth lenedd.

I have wended (turned) into English
Gospel's holy lore,
After the little wit that me
My Lord hath lent.

Other famous writers of English between this time and the appearance of Chaucer were Robert of Gloucester and Robert of Brunne, both of whom wrote Chronicles of England in verse.

CHAPTER II.

THE FOURTEENTH CENTURY.

1. The opening of the fourteenth century saw the death of the great and able king, Edward I., the "Hammer of the Scots," the "Keeper of his word." The century itself— a most eventful period— witnessed the feeble and disastrous reign of Edward II.; the long and prosperous rule— for fifty years— of Edward III.; the troubled times of Richard II., who exhibited almost a repetition of the faults of Edward II.; and the appearance of a new and powerful dynasty— the House of Lancaster— in the person of the able and ambitious Henry IV. This century saw also many striking events, and many still more striking changes. It beheld the welding of the Saxon and the Norman elements into one— chiefly through the French wars; the final triumph of the English language over French in 1362; the frequent coming of the Black Death; the victories of Crecy and Poitiers; it learned the universal use of the mariner's compass; it witnessed two kings— of France and of Scotland— prisoners in London; great changes in the condition of labourers; the invention of gunpowder in 1340; the rise of English commerce under Edward III.; and everywhere in England the rising up of new powers and new ideas.

2. The first prose-writer in this century is Sir John Mandeville (who has been called the "Father of English Prose"). King Alfred has also been called by this name; but as the English written by Alfred was very different from that written by Mandeville,— the latter containing a large admixture of French and of Latin words, both writers are deserving of the epithet. The most influential prose-writer was John Wyclif, who was, in fact, the first English Reformer of the Church. In poetry, two writers stand opposite each other in striking contrast— Geoffrey Chaucer and William Langlande, the first writing in courtly "King's English" in end-rhyme, and with the fullest inspirations from the literatures of France and Italy, the latter writing in head-rhyme, and— though using more French words than Chaucer— with a style that was always homely, plain, and pedestrian. John Gower, in Kent, and John Barbour, in Scotland, are also noteworthy poets in this century. The English language reached a high state of polish, power, and freedom in this period; and the sweetness and music of Chaucer's verse are still unsurpassed by modern poets. The sentences of the prose-writers of this century are long, clumsy, and somewhat helpless; but the sweet homely English rhythm exists in many of them, and was continued, through Wyclif's version, down into our translation of the Bible in 1611.

3. SIR JOHN MANDEVILLE, (1300-1372), "the first prose-writer in formed English," was born at St Albans, in Hertfordshire, in the year 1300. He was a physician; but, in the year 1322, he set out on a journey to the East; was away from home for more than thirty years, and died at Liège, in Belgium, in 1372. He wrote his travels first in Latin, next in French, and then turned them into English, "that every man of my nation may understand it." The book is a kind of guide-book to the Holy Land; but the writer himself went much further

east— reached Cathay or China, in fact. He introduced a large number of French words into our speech, such as cause, contrary, discover, quantity, and many hundred others. His works were much admired, read, and copied; indeed, hundreds of manuscript copies of his book were made. There are nineteen still in the British Museum. The book was not printed till the year 1499— that is, twenty-five years after printing was introduced into this country. Many of the Old English inflexions still survive in his style. Thus he says: "Machamete was born in Arabye, that was a pore knave (boy) that kepte cameles that wenten with marchantes for marchandise."

4. JOHN WYCLIF (his name is spelled in about forty different ways)— 1324-1384— was born at Hipswell, near Richmond, in Yorkshire, in the year 1324, and died at the vicarage of Lutterworth, in Leicestershire, in 1384. His fame rests on two bases— his efforts as a reformer of the abuses of the Church, and his complete translation of the Bible. This work was finished in 1383, just one year before his death. But the translation was not done by himself alone; the larger part of the Old Testament version seems to have been made by Nicholas de Hereford. Though often copied in manuscript, it was not printed for several centuries. Wyclif's New Testament was printed in 1731, and the Old Testament not until the year 1850. But the words and the style of his translation, which was read and re-read by hundreds of thoughtful men, were of real and permanent service in fixing the language in the form in which we now find it.

5. JOHN GOWER (1325-1408) was a country gentleman of Kent. As Mandeville wrote his travels in three languages, so did Gower his poems. Almost all educated persons in the fourteenth century could read and write with tolerable and with almost equal ease, English, French, and Latin. His three poems are the Speculum Meditantis ("The Mirror of the Thoughtful Man"), in French; the Vox Clamantis ("Voice of One Crying"), in Latin; and Confessio Amantis ("The Lover's Confession"), in English. No manuscript of the first work is known to exist. He was buried in St Saviour's, Southwark, where his effigy is still to be seen— his head resting on his three works. Chaucer called him "the moral Gower"; and his books are very dull, heavy, and difficult to read.

6. WILLIAM LANGLANDE (1332-1400), a poet who used the old English head-rhyme, as Chaucer used the foreign end-rhyme, was born at Cleobury-Mortimer in Shropshire, in the year 1332. The date of his death is doubtful. His poem is called the Vision of Piers the Plowman; and it is the last long poem in our literature that was written in Old English alliterative rhyme. From this period, if rhyme is employed at all, it is the end-rhyme, which we borrowed from the French and Italians. The poem has an appendix called Do-well, Do-bet, Do-best— the three stages in the growth of a Christian. Langlande's writings remained in manuscript until the reign of Edward VI.; they were printed then, and went through three editions in one year. The English used in the Vision is the Midland dialect— much the same as that used by Chaucer; only, oddly enough, Langlande admits into his English a larger amount of French words than Chaucer. The poem is a distinct landmark in the history of our speech. The

following is a specimen of the lines. There are three alliterative words in each line, with a pause near the middle—

"A voice {l}oud in that {l}ight · to {L}ucifer crïed,
'{P}rinces of this {p}alace · {p}rest[16] undo the gatës,
For here {c}ometh with {c}rown · the {k}ing of all glory!'"

[16: Quickly.]

7. GEOFFREY CHAUCER (1340-1400), the "father of English poetry," and the greatest narrative poet of this country, was born in London in or about the year 1340. He lived in the reigns of Edward III., Richard II., and one year in the reign of Henry IV. His father was a vintner. The name Chaucer is a Norman name, and is found on the roll of Battle Abbey. He is said to have studied both at Oxford and Cambridge; served as page in the household of Prince Lionel, Duke of Clarence, the third son of Edward III.; served also in the army, and was taken prisoner in one of the French campaigns. In 1367, he was appointed gentleman-in-waiting (valettus) to Edward III., who sent him on several embassies. In 1374 he married a lady of the Queen's chamber; and by this marriage he became connected with John of Gaunt, who afterwards married a sister of this lady. While on an embassy to Italy, he is reported to have met the great poet Petrarch, who told him the story of the Patient Griselda. In 1381, he was made Comptroller of Customs in the great port of London— an office which he held till the year 1386. In that year he was elected knight of the shire— that is, member of Parliament for the county of Kent. In 1389, he was appointed Clerk of the King's Works at Westminster and Windsor. From 1381 to 1389 was probably the best and most productive period of his life; for it was in this period that he wrote the House of Fame, the Legend of Good Women, and the best of the Canterbury Tales. From 1390 to 1400 was spent in writing the other Canterbury Tales, ballads, and some moral poems. He died at Westminster in the year 1400, and was the first writer who was buried in the Poets' Corner of the Abbey. We see from his life— and it was fortunate for his poetry— that Chaucer had the most varied experience as student, courtier, soldier, ambassador, official, and member of Parliament; and was able to mix freely and on equal terms with all sorts and conditions of men, from the king to the poorest hind in the fields. He was a stout man, with a small bright face, soft eyes, dazed by long and hard reading, and with the English passion for flowers, green fields, and all the sights and sounds of nature.

8. Chaucer's Works.— Chaucer's greatest work is the Canterbury Tales. It is a collection of stories written in heroic metre— that is, in the rhymed couplet of five iambic feet. The finest part of the Canterbury Tales is the Prologue; the noblest story is probably the Knightes Tale. It is worthy of note that, in 1362, when Chaucer was a very young man, the session of the House of Commons was first opened with a speech in English; and in the same year an Act of Parliament was passed, substituting the use of English for French in courts of law, in schools, and in public offices. English had thus triumphed over French in

all parts of the country, while it had at the same time become saturated with French words. In the year 1383 the Bible was translated into English by Wyclif. Thus Chaucer, whose writings were called by Spenser "the well of English undefiled," wrote at a time when our English was freshest and newest. The grammar of his works shows English with a large number of inflexions still remaining. The Canterbury Tales are a series of stories supposed to be told by a number of pilgrims who are on their way to the shrine of St Thomas (Becket) at Canterbury. The pilgrims, thirty-two in number, are fully described— their dress, look, manners, and character in the Prologue. It had been agreed, when they met at the Tabard Inn in Southwark, that each pilgrim should tell four stories— two going and two returning— as they rode along the grassy lanes, then the only roads, to the old cathedral city. But only four-and-twenty stories exist.

9. Chaucer's Style.— Chaucer expresses, in the truest and liveliest way, "the true and lively of everything which is set before him;" and he first gave to English poetry that force, vigour, life, and colour which raised it above the level of mere rhymed prose. All the best poems and histories in Latin, French, and Italian were well known to Chaucer; and he borrows from them with the greatest freedom. He handles, with masterly power, all the characters and events in his Tales; and he is hence, beyond doubt, the greatest narrative poet that England ever produced. In the Prologue, his masterpiece, Dryden says, "we have our forefathers and great-grand-dames all before us, as they were in Chaucer's days." His dramatic power, too, is nearly as great as his narrative power; and Mr Marsh affirms that he was "a dramatist before that which is technically known as the existing drama had been invented." That is to say, he could set men and women talking as they would and did talk in real life, but with more point, spirit, verve, and picturesqueness. As regards the matter of his poems, it may be sufficient to say that Dryden calls him "a perpetual fountain of good sense;" and that Hazlitt makes this remark: "Chaucer was the most practical of all the great poets,— the most a man of business and of the world. His poetry reads like history." Tennyson speaks of him thus in his "Dream of Fair Women":—

"Dan Chaucer, the first warbler, whose sweet breath
  Preluded those melodious bursts that fill
The spacious times of great Elizabeth,
  With sounds that echo still."

10. JOHN BARBOUR (1316-1396).— The earliest Scottish poet of any importance in the fourteenth century is John Barbour, who rose to be Archdeacon of Aberdeen. Barbour was of Norman blood, and wrote Northern English, or, as it is sometimes called, Scotch. He studied both at Oxford and at the University of Paris. His chief work is a poem called The Bruce. The English of this poem does not differ very greatly from the English of Chaucer. Barbour has fechtand for fighting; pressit for pressed; theretill for thereto; but these differences do not make the reading of his poem very difficult. As a Norman he was proud of the doings of Robert de Bruce, another Norman; and Barbour

must often have heard stories of him in his boyhood, as he was only thirteen when Bruce died.

CHAPTER III.

THE FIFTEENTH CENTURY.

1. The fifteenth century, a remarkable period in many ways, saw three royal dynasties established in England— the Houses of Lancaster, York, and Tudor. Five successful French campaigns of Henry V., and the battle of Agincourt; and, on the other side, the loss of all our large possessions in France, with the exception of Calais, under the rule of the weak Henry VI., were among the chief events of the fifteenth century. The Wars of the Roses did not contribute anything to the prosperity of the century, nor could so unsettled and quarrelsome a time encourage the cultivation of literature. For this among other reasons, we find no great compositions in prose or verse; but a considerable activity in the making and distribution of ballads. The best of these are Sir Patrick Spens, Edom o' Gordon, The Nut-Brown Mayde, and some of those written about Robin Hood and his exploits. The ballad was everywhere popular; and minstrels sang them in every city and village through the length and breadth of England. The famous ballad of Chevy Chase is generally placed after the year 1460, though it did not take its present form till the seventeenth century. It tells the story of the Battle of Otterburn, which was fought in 1388. This century was also witness to the short struggle of Richard III., followed by the rise of the House of Tudor. And, in 1498, just at its close, the wonderful apparition of a new world— of The New World— rose on the horizon of the English mind, for England then first heard of the discovery of America. But, as regards thinking and writing, the fifteenth century is the most barren in our literature. It is the most barren in the production of original literature; but, on the other hand, it is, compared with all the centuries that preceded it, the most fertile in the dissemination and distribution of the literature that already existed. For England saw, in the memorable year of 1474, the establishment of the first printing-press in the Almonry at Westminster, by William Caxton. The first book printed by him in this country was called 'The Game and Playe of the Chesse.' When Edward IV. and his friends visited Caxton's house and looked at his printing-press, they spoke of it as a pretty toy; they could not foresee that it was destined to be a more powerful engine of good government and the spread of thought and education than the Crown, Parliaments, and courts of law all put together. The two greatest names in literature in the fifteenth century are those of James I. (of Scotland) and William Caxton himself. Two followers of Chaucer, Occleve and Lydgate are also generally mentioned. Put shortly, one might say that the chief poetical productions of this century were its ballads; and the chief prose productions, translations from Latin or from foreign works.

2. JAMES I. OF SCOTLAND (1394-1437), though a Scotchman, owed his education to England. He was born in 1394. Whilst on his way to France when a boy of eleven, he was captured, in time of peace, by the order of Henry IV., and kept prisoner in England for about eighteen years. It was no great misfortune, for he received from Henry the best education that England could then give in

language, literature, music, and all knightly accomplishments. He married Lady Jane Beaufort, the grand-daughter of John of Gaunt, the friend and patron of Chaucer. His best and longest poem is The Kings Quair (that is, Book), a poem which was inspired by the subject of it, Lady Jane Beaufort herself. The poem is written in a stanza of seven lines (called Rime Royal); and the style is a close copy of the style of Chaucer. After reigning thirteen years in Scotland, King James was murdered at Perth, in the year 1437. A Norman by blood, he is the best poet of the fifteenth century.

3. WILLIAM CAXTON (1422-1492) is the name of greatest importance and significance in the history of our literature in the fifteenth century. He was born in Kent in the year 1422. He was not merely a printer, he was also a literary man; and, when he devoted himself to printing, he took to it as an art, and not as a mere mechanical device. Caxton in early life was a mercer in the city of London; and in the course of his business, which was a thriving one, he had to make frequent journeys to the Low Countries. Here he saw the printing-press for the first time, with the new separate types, was enchanted with it, and fired by the wonderful future it opened. It had been introduced into Holland about the year 1450. Caxton's press was set up in the Almonry at Westminster, at the sign of the Red Pole. It produced in all sixty-four books, nearly all of them in English, some of them written by Caxton himself. One of the most important of them was Sir Thomas Malory's History of King Arthur, the storehouse from which Tennyson drew the stories which form the groundwork of his Idylls of the King.

CHAPTER IV.

THE SIXTEENTH CENTURY.

1. The Wars of the Roses ended in 1485, with the victory of Bosworth Field. A new dynasty— the House of Tudor— sat upon the throne of England; and with it a new reign of peace and order existed in the country, for the power of the king was paramount, and the power of the nobles had been gradually destroyed in the numerous battles of the fifteenth century. Like the fifteenth, this century also is famous for its ballads, the authors of which are not known, but which seem to have been composed "by the people for the people." They were sung everywhere, at fairs and feasts, in town and country, at going to and coming home from work; and many of them were set to popular dance-tunes.

"When Tom came home from labour,
  And Cis from milking rose,
Merrily went the tabor,
  And merrily went their toes."

The ballads of King Lear and The Babes in the Wood are perhaps to be referred to this period.

2. The first half of the sixteenth century saw the beginning of a new era in poetry; and the last half saw the full meridian splendour of this new era. The beginning of this era was marked by the appearance of Sir Thomas Wyatt (1503-1542), and of the Earl of Surrey (1517-1547). These two eminent writers have been called the "twin-stars of the dawn," the "founders of English lyrical poetry"; and it is worthy of especial note, that it is to Wyatt that we owe the introduction of the Sonnet into our literature, and to Surrey that is due the introduction of Blank Verse. The most important prose-writers of the first half of the century were Sir Thomas More, the great lawyer and statesman, and William Tyndale, who translated the New Testament into English. In the latter half of the century, the great poets are Spenser and Shakespeare; the great prose-writers, Richard Hooker and Francis Bacon.

3. SIR THOMAS MORE'S (1480-1535) chief work in English is the Life and Reign of Edward V. It is written in a plain, strong, nervous English style. Hallam calls it "the first example of good English— pure and perspicuous, well chosen, without vulgarisms, and without pedantry." His Utopia (a description of the country of Nowhere) was written in Latin.

4. WILLIAM TYNDALE (1484-1536)— a man of the greatest significance, both in the history of religion, and in the history of our language and literature— was a native of Gloucestershire, and was educated at Magdalen Hall, Oxford. His opinions on religion and the rule of the Catholic Church, compelled him to leave England, and drove him to the Continent in the year 1523. He lived in Hamburg for some time. With the German and Swiss reformers he held that the Bible should be in the hands of every grown-up person, and not in the

exclusive keeping of the Church. He accordingly set to work to translate the Scriptures into his native tongue. Two editions of his version of the New Testament were printed in 1525-34. He next translated the five books of Moses, and the book of Jonah. In 1535 he was, after many escapes and adventures, finally tracked and hunted down by an emissary of the Pope's faction, and thrown into prison at the castle of Vilvoorde, near Brussels. In 1536 he was brought to Antwerp, tried, condemned, led to the stake, strangled, and burned.

5. The Work of William Tyndale.— Tyndale's translation has, since the time of its appearance, formed the basis of all the after versions of the Bible. It is written in the purest and simplest English; and very few of the words used in his translation have grown obsolete in our modern speech. Tyndale's work is indeed, one of the most striking landmarks in the history of our language. Mr Marsh says of it: "Tyndale's translation of the New Testament is the most important philological monument of the first half of the sixteenth century,— perhaps I should say, of the whole period between Chaucer and Shakespeare.... The best features of the translation of 1611 are derived from the version of Tyndale." It may be said without exaggeration that, in the United Kingdom, America, and the colonies, about one hundred millions of people now speak the English of Tyndale's Bible; nor is there any book that has exerted so great an influence on English rhythm, English style, the selection of words, and the build of sentences in our English prose.

6. EDMUND SPENSER (1552-1599), "The Poet's Poet," and one of the greatest poetical writers of his own or of any age, was born at East Smithfield, near the Tower of London, in the year 1552, about nine years before the birth of Bacon, and in the reign of Edward VI. He was educated at Merchant Taylors' School in London, and at Pembroke Hall, Cambridge. In 1579, we find him settled in his native city, where his best friend was the gallant Sir Philip Sidney, who introduced him to his uncle, the Earl of Leicester, then at the height of his power and influence with Queen Elizabeth. In the same year was published his first poetical work, The Shepheard's Calendar— a set of twelve pastoral poems. In 1580, he went to Ireland as Secretary to Lord Grey de Wilton, the Viceroy of that country. For some years he resided at Kilcolman Castle, in county Cork, on an estate which had been granted him out of the forfeited lands of the Earl of Desmond. Sir Walter Raleigh had obtained a similar but larger grant, and was Spenser's near neighbour. In 1590 Spenser brought out the first three books of The Faerie Queene. The second three books of his great poem appeared in 1596. Towards the end of 1598, a rebellion broke out in Ireland; it spread into Munster; Spenser's house was attacked and set on fire; in the fighting and confusion his only son perished; and Spenser escaped with the greatest difficulty. In deep distress of body and mind, he made his way to London, where he died— at an inn in King Street, Westminster, at the age of forty-six, in the beginning of the year 1599. He was buried in the Abbey, not far from the grave of Chaucer.

7. Spenser's Style.— His greatest work is The Faerie Queene; but that in which he shows the most striking command of language is his Hymn of

Heavenly Love. The Faerie Queene is written in a nine-lined stanza, which has since been called the Spenserian Stanza. The first eight lines are of the usual length of five iambic feet; the last line contains six feet, and is therefore an Alexandrine. Each stanza contains only three rhymes, which are disposed in this order: a b a b b c b c c. —The music of the stanza is long-drawn out, beautiful, involved, and even luxuriant. —The story of the poem is an allegory, like the 'Pilgrim's Progress'; and in it Spenser undertook, he says, "to represent all the moral virtues, assigning to every virtue a knight to be the patron and defender of the same."[17] Only six books were completed; and these relate the adventures of the knights who stand for Holiness, Temperance, Chastity, Friendship, Justice, and Courtesy. The Faerie Queene herself is called Gloriana, who represents Glory in his "general intention," and Queen Elizabeth in his "particular intention."

[17: This use of the phrase "the same" is antiquated English.]

8. Character of the Faerie Queene.— This poem is the greatest of the sixteenth century. Spenser has not only been the delight of nearly ten generations; he was the study of Shakespeare, the poetical master of Cowley and of Milton, and, in some sense, of Dryden and Pope. Keats, when a boy, was never tired of reading him. "There is something," says Pope, "in Spenser that pleases one as strongly in old age as it did in one's youth." Professor Craik says: "Without calling Spenser the greatest of all poets, we may still say that his poetry is the most poetical of all poetry." The outburst of national feeling after the defeat of the Armada in 1588; the new lands opened up by our adventurous Devonshire sailors; the strong and lively loyalty of the nation to the queen; the great statesmen and writers of the period; the high daring shown by England against Spain— all these animated and inspired the glowing genius of Spenser. His rhythm is singularly sweet and beautiful. Hazlitt says: "His versification is at once the most smooth and the most sounding in the language. It is a labyrinth of sweet sounds." Nothing can exceed the wealth of Spenser's phrasing and expression; there seems to be no limit to its flow. He is very fond of the Old-English practice of alliteration or head-rhyme— "hunting the letter," as it was called. Thus he has—

"In woods, in waves, in wars, she wont to dwell.
Gay without good is good heart's greatest loathing."

9. WILLIAM SHAKESPEARE (1564-1616), the greatest dramatist that England ever produced, was born at Stratford-on-Avon, in Warwickshire, on the 23d of April— St George's Day— of the year 1564. His father, John Shakespeare, was a wool dealer and grower. William was educated at the grammar-school of the town, where he learned "small Latin and less Greek"; and this slender stock was his only scholastic outfit for life. At the early age of eighteen he married Anne Hathaway, a yeoman's daughter. In 1586, at the age of twenty-two, he quitted his native town, and went to London.

10. Shakespeare's Life and Character.— He was employed in some menial capacity at the Blackfriars Theatre, but gradually rose to be actor and also adapter of plays. He was connected with the theatre for about five-and-twenty

years; and so diligent and so successful was he, that he was able to purchase shares both in his own theatre and in the Globe. As an actor, he was only second-rate: the two parts he is known to have played are those of the Ghost in Hamlet, and Adam in As You Like It. In 1597, at the early age of thirty-three, he was able to purchase New Place, in Stratford, and to rebuild the house. In 1612, at the age of forty-eight, he left London altogether, and retired for the rest of his life to New Place, where he died in the year 1616. His old father and mother spent the last years of their lives with him, and died under his roof. Shakespeare had three children— two girls and a boy. The boy, Hamnet, died at the age of twelve. Shakespeare himself was beloved by every one who knew him; and "gentle Shakespeare" was the phrase most often upon the lips of his friends. A placid face, with a sweet, mild expression; a high, broad, noble, "two-storey" forehead; bright eyes; a most speaking mouth— though it seldom opened; an open, frank manner, a kindly, handsome look,— such seems to have been the external character of the man Shakespeare.

11. Shakespeare's Works.— He has written thirty-seven plays and many poems. The best of his rhymed poems are his Sonnets, in which he chronicles many of the various moods of his mind. The plays consist of tragedies, historical plays, and comedies. The greatest of his tragedies are probably Hamlet and King Lear; the best of his historical plays, Richard III. and Julius Cæsar; and his finest comedies, Midsummer Night's Dream and As You Like It. He wrote in the reign of Elizabeth as well as in that of James; but his greatest works belong to the latter period.

12. Shakespeare's Style.— Every one knows that Shakespeare is great; but how is the young learner to discover the best way of forming an adequate idea of his greatness? In the first place, Shakespeare has very many sides; and, in the second place, he is great on every one of them. Coleridge says: "In all points, from the most important to the most minute, the judgment of Shakespeare is commensurate with his genius— nay, his genius reveals itself in his judgment, as in its most exalted form." He has been called "mellifluous Shakespeare;" "honey-tongued Shakespeare;" "silver-tongued Shakespeare;" "the thousand-souled Shakespeare;" "the myriad-minded;" and by many other epithets. He seems to have been master of all human experience; to have known the human heart in all its phases; to have been acquainted with all sorts and conditions of men— high and low, rich and poor; and to have studied the history of past ages, and of other countries. He also shows a greater and more highly skilled mastery over language than any other writer that ever lived. The vocabulary employed by Shakespeare amounts in number of words to twenty-one thousand. The vocabulary of Milton numbers only seven thousand words. But it is not sufficient to say that Shakespeare's power of thought, of feeling, and of expression required three times the number of words to express itself; we must also say that Shakespeare's power of expression shows infinitely greater skill, subtlety, and cunning than is to be found in the works of Milton. Shakespeare had also a marvellous power of making new phrases, most of which have become part and parcel of our language. Such phrases as every inch a king; witch the world; the time is out of

joint, and hundreds more, show that modern Englishmen not only speak Shakespeare, but think Shakespeare. His knowledge of human nature has enabled him to throw into English literature a larger number of genuine "characters" that will always live in the thoughts of men, than any other author that ever wrote. And he has not drawn his characters from England alone and from his own time— but from Greece and Rome, from other countries, too, and also from all ages. He has written in a greater variety of styles than any other writer. "Shakespeare," says Professor Craik, "has invented twenty styles." The knowledge, too, that he shows on every kind of human endeavour is as accurate as it is varied. Lawyers say that he was a great lawyer; theologians, that he was an able divine, and unequalled in his knowledge of the Bible; printers, that he must have been a printer; and seamen, that he knew every branch of the sailor's craft.

13. Shakespeare's contemporaries.— But we are not to suppose that Shakespeare stood alone in the end of the sixteenth and the beginning of the seventeenth century as a great poet; and that everything else was flat and low around him. This never is and never can be the case. Great genius is the possession, not of one man, but of several in a great age; and we do not find a great writer standing alone and unsupported, just as we do not find a high mountain rising from a low plain. The largest group of the highest mountains in the world, the Himalayas, rise from the highest table-land in the world; and peaks nearly as high as the highest— Mount Everest— are seen cleaving the blue sky in the neighbourhood of Mount Everest itself. And so we find Shakespeare surrounded by dramatists in some respects nearly as great as himself; for the same great forces welling up within the heart of England that made him created also the others. Marlowe, the teacher of Shakespeare, Peele, and Greene, preceded him; Ben Jonson, Beaumont and Fletcher, Massinger and Ford, Webster, Chapman, and many others, were his contemporaries, lived with him, talked with him; and no doubt each of these men influenced the work of the others. But the works of these men belong chiefly to the seventeenth century. We must not, however, forget that the reign of Queen Elizabeth— called in literature the Elizabethan Period— was the greatest that England ever saw,— greatest in poetry and in prose, greatest in thought and in action, perhaps also greatest in external events.

14. CHRISTOPHER MARLOWE (1564-1593), the first great English dramatist, was born at Canterbury in the year 1564, two months before the birth of Shakespeare himself. He studied at Corpus Christi College, Cambridge, and took the degree of Master of Arts in 1587. After leaving the university, he came up to London and wrote for the stage. He seems to have led a wild and reckless life, and was stabbed in a tavern brawl on the 1st of June 1593. "As he may be said to have invented and made the verse of the drama, so he created the English drama." His chief plays are Dr Faustus and Edward the Second. His style is one of the greatest vigour and power: it is often coarse, but it is always strong. Ben Jonson spoke of "Marlowe's mighty line"; and Lord Jeffrey says of him: "In felicity of thought and strength of expression, he is second only to Shakespeare himself."

15. BEN JONSON (1574-1637), the greatest dramatist of England after Shakespeare, was born in Westminster in the year 1574, just nine years after Shakespeare's birth. He received his education at Westminster School. It is said that, after leaving school, he was obliged to assist his stepfather as a bricklayer; that he did not like the work; and that he ran off to the Low Countries, and there enlisted as a soldier. On his return to London, he began to write for the stage. Jonson was a friend and companion of Shakespeare's; and at the Mermaid, in Fleet Street, they had, in presence of men like Raleigh, Marlowe, Greene, Peele, and other distinguished Englishmen, many "wit-combats" together. Jonson's greatest plays are Volpone or the Fox, and the Alchemist— both comedies. In 1616 he was created Poet-Laureate. For many years he was in receipt of a pension from James I. and from Charles I.; but so careless and profuse were his habits, that he died in poverty in the year 1637. He was buried in an upright position in Westminster Abbey; and the stone over his grave still bears the inscription, "O rare Ben Jonson!" He has been called a "robust, surly, and observing dramatist."

16. RICHARD HOOKER (1553-1600), one of the greatest of Elizabethan prose-writers, was born at Heavitree, a village near the city of Exeter, in the year 1553. By the kind aid of Jewel, Bishop of Salisbury, he was sent to Oxford, where he distinguished himself as a hard-working student, and especially for his knowledge of Hebrew. In 1581 he entered the Church. In the same year he made an imprudent marriage with an ignorant, coarse, vulgar, and domineering woman. He was appointed Master of the Temple in 1585; but, by his own request, he was removed from that office, and chose the quieter living of Boscombe, near Salisbury. Here he wrote the first four books of his famous work, The Laws of Ecclesiastical Polity, which were published in the year 1594. In 1595 he was translated to the living of Bishopsborne, near Canterbury. His death took place in the year 1600. The complete work, which consisted of eight books, was not published till 1662.

17. Hooker's Style.— His writings are said to "mark an era in English prose." His sentences are generally very long, very elaborate, but full of "an extraordinary musical richness of language." The order is often more like that of a Latin than of an English sentence; and he is fond of Latin inversions. Thus he writes: "That which by wisdom he saw to be requisite for that people, was by as great wisdom compassed." The following sentences give us a good example of his sweet and musical rhythm. "Of law there can be no less acknowledged, than that her seat is the bosom of God, her voice the harmony of the world. All things in heaven and earth do her homage; the very least as feeling her care, and the greatest as not exempted from her power: both angels and men, and creatures of what condition soever, though each in different sort and manner, yet all, with uniform consent, admiring her as the mother of their peace and joy."

18. SIR PHILIP SIDNEY (1554-1586), a noble knight, a statesman, and one of the best prose-writers of the Elizabethan age, was born at Penshurst, in Kent, in the year 1554. He was educated at Shrewsbury School, and then at Christ

Church, Oxford. At the age of seventeen he went abroad for three years' travel on the Continent; and, while in Paris, witnessed, from the windows of the English Embassy, the horrible Massacre of St Bartholomew in the year 1572. At the early age of twenty-two he was sent as ambassador to the Emperor of Germany; and while on that embassy, he met William of Orange— "William the Silent"— who pronounced him one of the ripest statesmen in Europe. This was said of a young man "who seems to have been the type of what was noblest in the youth of England during times that could produce a statesman." In 1580 he wrote the Arcadia, a romance, and dedicated it to his sister, the Countess of Pembroke. The year after, he produced his Apologie for Poetrie. His policy as a statesman was to side with Protestant rulers, and to break the power of the strongest Catholic kingdom on the Continent— the power of Spain. In 1585 the Queen sent him to the Netherlands as governor of the important fortress of Flushing. He was mortally wounded in a skirmish at Zutphen; and as he was being carried off the field, handed to a private the cup of cold water that had been brought to quench his raging thirst. He died of his wounds on the 17th of October 1586. One of his friends wrote of him:—
"Death, courage, honour, make thy soul to live!—
Thy soul in heaven, thy name in tongues of men!"

19. Sidney's Poetry.— In addition to the Arcadia and the Apologie for Poetrie, Sidney wrote a number of beautiful poems. The best of these are a series of sonnets called Astrophel and Stella, of which his latest critic says: "As a series of sonnets, the Astrophel and Stella poems are second only to Shakespeare's; as a series of love-poems, they are perhaps unsurpassed." Spenser wrote an elegy upon Sidney himself, under the title of Astrophel. Sidney's prose is among the best of the sixteenth century. "He reads more modern than any other author of that century." He does not use "ink-horn terms," or cram his sentences with Latin or French or Italian words; but both his words and his idioms are of pure English. He is fond of using personifications. Such phrases as, "About the time that the candles began to inherit the sun's office;" "Seeing the day begin to disclose her comfortable beauties," are not uncommon. The rhythm of his sentences is always melodious, and each of them has a very pleasant close.

CHAPTER V.

THE SEVENTEENTH CENTURY.

1. The First Half.— Under the wise and able rule of Queen Elizabeth, this country had enjoyed a long term of peace. The Spanish Armada had been defeated in 1588; the Spanish power had gradually waned before the growing might of England; and it could be said with perfect truth, in the words of Shakespeare:—

"In her days every man doth eat in safety
Under his own vine what he plants, and sing
The merry songs of peace to all his neighbours."

The country was at peace; and every peaceful art and pursuit prospered. As one sign of the great prosperity and outstretching enterprise of commerce, we should note the foundation of the East India Company on the last day of the year 1600. The reign of James I. (1603-1625) was also peaceful; and the country made steady progress in industries, in commerce, and in the arts and sciences. The two greatest prose-writers of the first half of the seventeenth century were Raleigh and Bacon; the two greatest poets were Shakespeare and Ben Jonson.

2. SIR WALTER RALEIGH (1552-1618).— Walter Raleigh, soldier, statesman, coloniser, historian, and poet, was born in Devonshire, in the year 1552. He was sent to Oriel College, Oxford; but he left at the early age of seventeen to fight on the side of the Protestants in France. From that time his life is one long series of schemes, plots, adventures, and misfortunes— culminating in his execution at Westminster in the year 1618. He spent "the evening of a tempestuous life" in the Tower, where he lay for thirteen years; and during this imprisonment he wrote his greatest work, the History of the World, which was never finished. His life and adventures belong to the sixteenth; his works to the seventeenth century. Raleigh was probably the most dazzling figure of his time; and is "in a singular degree the representative of the vigorous versatility of the Elizabethan period." Spenser, whose neighbour he was for some time in Ireland, thought highly of his poetry, calls him "the summer's nightingale," and says of him—

"Yet æmuling[18] my song, he took in hand
  My pipe, before that æmulèd of many,
And played thereon (for well that skill he conn'd),
  Himself as skilful in that art as any."

Raleigh is the author of the celebrated verses, "Go, soul, the body's guest;" "Give me my scallop-shell of quiet;" and of the lines which were written and left in his Bible on the night before he was beheaded:—

"Even such is time, that takes in trust
Our youth, our joys, our all we have,
And pays us but with age and dust;
Who, in the dark and silent grave,
When we have wandered all our ways,
Shuts up the story of our days:
But from this earth, this grave, this dust,
The Lord shall raise me up, I trust!"

Raleigh's prose has been described as "some of the most flowing and modern-looking prose of the period;" and there can be no doubt that, if he had given himself entirely to literature, he would have been one of the greatest poets and prose-writers of his time. His style is calm, noble, and melodious. The following is the last sentence of the History of the World:—

"O eloquent, just, and mighty Death! whom none could advise, thou
hast persuaded; what none hath dared, thou hast done; and whom all
the world hath flattered, thou only hast cast out of the world and
despised; thou hast drawn together all the far-stretched greatness,
all the pride, cruelty, and ambition of man, and covered it all over
with these two narrow words Hic jacet."

[18: Emulating.]

3. FRANCIS BACON (1561-1626), one of the greatest of English thinkers, and one of our best prose-writers, was born at York House, in the Strand, London, in the year 1561. He was a grave and precocious child; and Queen Elizabeth, who knew him and liked him, used to pat him and call him her "young Lord Keeper"— his father being Lord Keeper of the Seals in her reign. At the early age of twelve he was sent to Trinity College, Cambridge, and remained there for three years. In 1582 he was called to the bar; in 1593 he was M.P. for Middlesex. But his greatest rise in fortune did not take place till the reign of James I.; when, in the year 1618, he had risen to be Lord High Chancellor of England. The title which he took on this occasion— for the Lord High Chancellor is chairman of the House of Lords— was Baron Verulam; and a few years after he was created Viscount St Albans. His eloquence was famous in England; and Ben Jonson said of him: "The fear of every man that heard him was lest he should make an end." In the year 1621 he was accused of taking bribes, and of giving unjust decisions as a judge. He had not really been unconscientious, but he had been careless; was obliged to plead guilty; and he was sentenced to pay a fine of £40,000, and to be imprisoned in the Tower during the king's pleasure. The fine was remitted; Bacon was set free in two days; a pension was allowed him; but he never afterwards held office of any kind. He died on Easter-day of the year 1626, of a chill which he caught while experimenting on the preservative properties of snow.

4. His chief prose-works in English— for he wrote many in Latin— are the Essays, and the Advancement of Learning. His Essays make one of the wisest books ever written; and a great number of English thinkers owe to them the best of what they have had to say. They are written in a clear, forcible, pithy, and picturesque style, with short sentences, and a good many illustrations, drawn from history, politics, and science. It is true that the style is sometimes stiff, and even rigid; but the stiffness is the stiffness of a richly embroidered cloth, into which threads of gold and silver have been worked. Bacon kept what he called a Promus or Commonplace-Book; and in this he entered striking thoughts, sentences, and phrases that he met with in the course of his reading, or that occurred to him during the day. He calls these sentences "salt-pits, that you may extract salt out of, and sprinkle as you will." The following are a few examples:—

"That that is Forced is not Forcible."

"No Man loveth his Fetters though they be of Gold."

"Clear and Round Dealing is the Honour of Man's Nature."

"The Arch-flatterer, with whom all the petty Flatterers have intelligence, is a Man's Self."

"If Things be not tossed upon the Arguments of Counsell, they will be tossed upon the Waves of Fortune."

The following are a few striking sentences from his Essays:—

"Virtue is like a rich stone, best plain set."

"A man's nature runs either to herbs or weeds; therefore, let him seasonably water the one, and destroy the other."

"A crowd is not company, and faces are but a gallery of pictures, and talk but a tinkling cymbal, when there is no love."

No man could say wiser things in pithier words; and we may well say of his thoughts, in the words of Tennyson, that they are—

   "Jewels, five words long,
That on the stretched forefinger of all time
Sparkle for ever."

5. WILLIAM SHAKESPEARE (1564-1616) has been already treated of in the chapter on the sixteenth century. But it may be noted here that his first two periods— as they are called— fall within the sixteenth, and his last two periods within the seventeenth century. His first period lies between 1591 and 1596; and to it are ascribed his early poems, his play of Richard II., and some other historical plays. His second period, which stretches from 1596 to 1601 holds the Sonnets, the Merchant of Venice, the Merry Wives of Windsor, and a few historical dramas. But his third and fourth periods were richer in production, and in greater productions. The third period, which belongs to the years 1601 to 1608, produced the play of Julius Cæsar, the great tragedies of Hamlet, Othello, Lear, Macbeth, and some others. To the fourth period, which lies between 1608

and 1613, belong the calmer and wiser dramas,— Winter's Tale, The Tempest, and Henry VIII. Three years after— in 1616— he died.

6. The Second Half.— The second half of the great and unique seventeenth century was of a character very different indeed from that of the first half. The Englishmen born into it had to face a new world! New thoughts in religion, new forces in politics, new powers in social matters had been slowly, steadily, and irresistibly rising into supremacy ever since the Scottish King James came to take his seat upon the throne of England in 1603. These new forces had, in fact, become so strong that they led a king to the scaffold, and handed over the government of England to a section of Republicans. Charles I. was executed in 1649; and, though his son came back to the throne in 1660, the face, the manners, the thoughts of England and of Englishmen had undergone a complete internal and external change. The Puritan party was everywhere the ruling party; and its views and convictions, in religion, in politics, and in literature, held unquestioned sway in almost every part of England. In the Puritan party, the strongest section was formed by the Independents— the "root and branch men"— as they were called; and the greatest man among the Independents was Oliver Cromwell, in whose government John Milton was Foreign Secretary. Milton was certainly by far the greatest and most powerful writer, both in prose and in verse, on the side of the Puritan party. The ablest verse-writer on the Royalist or Court side was Samuel Butler, the unrivalled satirist— the Hogarth of language,— the author of Hudibras. The greatest prose-writer on the Royalist and Church side was Jeremy Taylor, Bishop of Down, in Ireland, and the author of Holy Living, Holy Dying, and many other works written with a wonderful eloquence. The greatest philosophical writer was Thomas Hobbes, the author of the Leviathan. The most powerful writer for the people was John Bunyan, the immortal author of The Pilgrim's Progress. When, however, we come to the reigns of Charles II. and James II., and the new influences which their rule and presence imparted, we find the greatest poet to be John Dryden, and the most important prose-writer, John Locke.

7. The Poetry of the Second Half.— The poetry of the second half of the seventeenth century was not an outgrowth or lineal descendant of the poetry of the first half. No trace of the strong Elizabethan poetical emotion remained; no writer of this half-century can claim kinship with the great authors of the Elizabethan period. The three most remarkable poets in the latter half of this century are John Milton, Samuel Butler, and John Dryden. But Milton's culture was derived chiefly from the great Greek and Latin writers; and his poems show few or no signs of belonging to any age or generation in particular of English literature. Butler's poem, the Hudibras, is the only one of its kind; and if its author owes anything to other writers, it is to France and not to England that we must look for its sources. Dryden, again, shows no sign of being related to Shakespeare or the dramatic writers of the early part of the century; he is separated from them by a great gulf; he owes most, when he owes anything, to the French school of poetry.

8. JOHN MILTON (1608-1674), the second greatest name in English poetry, and the greatest of all our epic poets, was born in Bread Street, Cheapside, London, in the year 1608— five years after the accession of James I. to the throne, and eight years before the death of Shakespeare. He was educated at St Paul's School, and then at Christ's College, Cambridge. He was so handsome— with a delicate complexion, clear blue eyes, and light-brown hair flowing down his shoulders— that he was known as the "Lady of Christ's." He was destined for the Church; but, being early seized with a strong desire to compose a great poetical work which should bring honour to his country and to the English tongue, he gave up all idea of becoming a clergyman. Filled with his secret purpose, he retired to Horton, in Buckinghamshire, where his father had bought a small country seat. Between the years 1632 and 1638 he studied all the best Greek and Latin authors, mathematics, and science; and he also wrote L'Allegro and Il Penseroso, Comus, Lycidas, and some shorter poems. These were preludes, or exercises, towards the great poetical work which it was the mission of his life to produce. In 1638-39 he took a journey to the Continent. Most of his time was spent in Italy; and, when in Florence, he paid a visit to Galileo in prison. It had been his intention to go on to Greece; but the troubled state of politics at home brought him back sooner than he wished. The next ten years of his life were engaged in teaching and in writing his prose works. His ideas on teaching are to be found in his Tractate on Education. The most eloquent of his prose-works is his Areopagitica, a Speech for the Liberty of Unlicensed Printing (1644)— a plea for the freedom of the press, for relieving all writings from the criticism of censors. In 1649— the year of the execution of Charles I.— Milton was appointed Latin or Foreign Secretary to the Government of Oliver Cromwell; and for the next ten years his time was taken up with official work, and with writing prose-volumes in defence of the action of the Republic. In 1660 the Restoration took place; and Milton was at length free, in his fifty-third year, to carry out his long-cherished scheme of writing a great Epic poem. He chose the subject of the fall and the restoration of man. Paradise Lost was completed in 1665; but, owing to the Plague and the Fire of London, it was not published till the year 1667. Milton's young Quaker friend, Ellwood, said to him one day: "Thou hast said much of Paradise Lost, what hast thou to say of Paradise Found?" Paradise Regained was the result— a work which was written in 1666, and appeared, along with Samson Agonistes, in the year 1671. Milton died in the year 1674— about the middle of the reign of Charles II. He had been three times married.

9. L'Allegro (or "The Cheerful Man") is a companion poem to Il Penseroso (or "The Meditative Man"). The poems present two contrasted views of the life of the student. They are written in an irregular kind of octosyllabic verse. The Comus— mostly in blank verse— is a lyrical drama; and Milton's work was accompanied by a musical composition by the then famous musician Henry Lawes. Lycidas— a poem in irregular rhymed verse— is a threnody on the death of Milton's young friend, Edward King, who was drowned in sailing from Chester to Dublin. This poem has been called "the touchstone of taste;" the

man who cannot admire it has no feeling for true poetry. The Paradise Lost is the story of how Satan was allowed to plot against the happiness of man; and how Adam and Eve fell through his designs. The style is the noblest in the English language; the music of the rhythm is lofty, involved, sustained, and sublime. "In reading 'Paradise Lost,'" says Mr Lowell, "one has a feeling of spaciousness such as no other poet gives." Paradise Regained is, in fact, the story of the Temptation, and of Christ's triumph over the wiles of Satan. Wordsworth says: "'Paradise Regained' is most perfect in execution of any written by Milton;" and Coleridge remarks that "it is in its kind the most perfect poem extant, though its kind may be inferior in interest." Samson Agonistes ("Samson in Struggle") is a drama, in highly irregular unrhymed verse, in which the poet sets forth his own unhappy fate—

"Eyeless, in Gaza, at the mill with slaves."

It is, indeed, an autobiographical poem— it is the story of the last years of the poet's life.

10. SAMUEL BUTLER (1612-1680), the wittiest of English poets, was born at Strensham, in Worcestershire, in the year 1612, four years after the birth of Milton, and four years before the death of Shakespeare. He was educated at the grammar-school of Worcester, and afterwards at Cambridge— but only for a short time. At the Restoration he was made secretary to the Earl of Carbery, who was then President of the Principality of Wales, and steward of Ludlow Castle. The first part of his long poem called Hudibras appeared in 1662; the second part in 1663; the third in 1678. Two years after, Butler died in the greatest poverty in London. He was buried in St Paul's, Covent Garden; but a monument was erected to him in Westminster Abbey. Upon this fact Wesley wrote the following epigram:—

"While Butler, needy wretch, was yet alive,
No generous patron would a dinner give;
See him, when starved to death, and turned to dust,
Presented with a monumental bust.
The poet's fate is here in emblem shown,—
He asked for bread, and he received a stone."

11. The Hudibras is a burlesque poem,— a long lampoon, a laboured caricature,— in mockery of the weaker side of the great Puritan party. It is an imaginary account of the adventures of a Puritan knight and his squire in the Civil Wars. It is choke-full of all kinds of learning, of the most pungent remarks— a very hoard of sentences and saws, "of vigorous locutions and picturesque phrases, of strong, sound sense, and robust English." It has been more quoted from than almost any book in our language. Charles II. was never tired of reading it and quoting from it—
"He never ate, nor drank, nor slept,
But Hudibras still near him kept"—
says Butler himself.

The following are some of his best known lines:—

"And, like a lobster boil'd, the morn
From black to red began to turn."

"For loyalty is still the same,
Whether it win or lose the game:
True as the dial to the sun,
Altho' it be not shin'd upon."

"He that complies against his will,
Is of his own opinion still."

12. JOHN DRYDEN (1631-1700), the greatest of our poets in the second rank, was born at Aldwincle, in Northamptonshire, in the year 1631. He was descended from Puritan ancestors on both sides of his house. He was educated at Westminster School, and at Trinity College, Cambridge. London became his settled abode in the year 1657. At the Restoration, in 1660, he became an ardent Royalist; and, in the year 1663, he married the daughter of a Royalist nobleman, the Earl of Berkshire. It was not a happy marriage; the lady, on the one hand, had a violent temper, and, on the other, did not care a straw for the literary pursuits of her husband. In 1666 he wrote his first long poem, the Annus Mirabilis ("The Wonderful Year"), in which he paints the war with Holland, and the Fire of London; and from this date his life is "one long literary labour." In 1670, he received the double appointment of Historiographer-Royal and Poet-Laureate. Up to the year 1681, his work lay chiefly in writing plays for the theatre; and these plays were written in rhymed verse, in imitation of the French plays; for, from the date of the Restoration, French influence was paramount both in literature and in fashion. But in this year he published the first part of Absalom and Achitophel— one of the most powerful satires in the language. In the year 1683 he was appointed Collector of Customs in the port of London— a post which Chaucer had held before him. (It is worthy of note that Dryden "translated" the Tales of Chaucer into modern English.) At the accession of James II., in 1685, Dryden became a Roman Catholic; most certainly neither for gain nor out of gratitude, but from conviction. In 1687, appeared his poem of The Hind and the Panther, in which he defends his new creed. He had, a few years before, brought out another poem called Religio Laici ("A Layman's Faith"), which was a defence of the Church of England and of her position in religion. In The Hind and the Panther, the Hind represents the Roman Catholic Church, "a milk-white hind, unspotted and unchanged," the Panther the Church of England; and the two beasts reply to each other in all the arguments used by controversialists on these two sides. When the Revolution of 1688 took place, and James II. had to flee the kingdom, Dryden lost both his offices and the pension he had from the Crown. Nothing daunted, he set to work once more. Again he wrote for the stage; but the last years of his life were spent chiefly in

translation. He translated passages from Homer, Ovid, and from some Italian writers; but his most important work was the translation of the whole of Virgil's Æneid. To the last he retained his fire and vigour, action and rush of verse; and some of his greatest lyric poems belong to his later years. His ode called Alexander's Feast was written at the age of sixty-six; and it was written at one sitting. At the age of sixty-nine he was meditating a translation of the whole of Homer— both the Iliad and the Odyssey. He died at his house in London, on May-day of 1700, and was buried with great pomp and splendour in Poets' Corner in Westminster Abbey.

13. His best satire is the Absalom and Achitophel; his best specimen of reasoning in verse is The Hind and the Panther. His best ode is his Ode to the Memory of Mrs Anne Killigrew. Dryden's style is distinguished by its power, sweep, vigour, and "long majestic march." No one has handled the heroic couplet— and it was this form of verse that he chiefly used— with more vigour than Dryden; Pope was more correct, more sparkling, more finished, but he had not Dryden's magnificent march or sweeping impulsiveness. "The fire and spirit of the 'Annus Mirabilis,'" says his latest critic, "are nothing short of amazing, when the difficulties which beset the author are remembered. The glorious dash of the performance is his own." His prose, though full of faults, is also very vigorous. It has "something of the lightning zigzag vigour and splendour of his verse." He always writes clear, homely, and pure English,— full of force and point.

Many of his most pithy lines are often quoted:—
"Men are but children of a larger growth."
"Errors, like straws, upon the surface flow;
He that would search for pearls must dive below."
"The greatest argument for love is love."
"The secret pleasure of the generous act,
Is the great mind's great bribe."

The great American critic and poet, Mr Lowell, compares him to "an ostrich, to be classed with flying things, and capable, what with leap and flap together, of leaving the earth for a longer or a shorter space, but loving the open plain, where wing and foot help each other to something that is both flight and run at once."

14. JEREMY TAYLOR (1613-1667), the greatest master of ornate and musical English prose in his own day, was born at Cambridge in the year 1613— just three years before Shakespeare died. His father was a barber. After attending the free grammar-school of Cambridge, he proceeded to the University. He took holy orders and removed to London. When he was lecturing one day at St Paul's, Archbishop Laud was so taken by his "youthful beauty, pleasant air," fresh eloquence, and exuberant style, that he had him created a Fellow of All Souls' College, Oxford. When the Civil War broke out, he was taken prisoner by the Parliamentary forces; and, indeed, suffered imprisonment more than once.

After the Restoration, he was presented with a bishopric in Ireland, where he died in 1667.

15. Perhaps his best works are his Holy Living and Holy Dying. His style is rich, even to luxury, full of the most imaginative illustrations, and often overloaded with ornament. He has been called "the Shakespeare of English prose," "the Spenser of divinity," and by other appellations. The latter title is a very happy description; for he has the same wealth of style, phrase, and description that Spenser has, and the same boundless delight in setting forth his thoughts in a thousand different ways. The following is a specimen of his writing. He is speaking of a shipwreck:—

"These are the thoughts of mortals, this is the end and sum of all
their designs. A dark night and an ill guide, a boisterous sea and a
broken cable, a hard rock and a rough wind, dash in pieces the
fortune of a whole family; and they that shall weep loudest for the
accident are not yet entered into the storm, and yet have suffered
shipwreck."

His writings contain many pithy statements. The following are a few of them:—

"No man is poor that does not think himself so."

"He that spends his time in sport and calls it recreation, is like
him whose garment is all made of fringe, and his meat nothing but
sauce."

"A good man is as much in awe of himself as of a whole assembly."

16. THOMAS HOBBES (1588-1679), a great philosopher, was born at Malmesbury in the year 1588. He is hence called "the philosopher of Malmesbury." He lived during the reigns of four English sovereigns— Elizabeth, James I., Charles I., and Charles II.; and he was twenty-eight years of age when Shakespeare died. He is in many respects the type of the hard-working, long-lived, persistent Englishman. He was for many years tutor in the Devonshire family— to the first Earl of Devonshire, and to the third Earl of Devonshire— and lived for several years at the family seat of Chatsworth. In his youth he was acquainted with Bacon and Ben Jonson; in his middle age he knew Galileo in Italy; and as he lived to the age of ninety-two, he might have conversed with John Locke or with Daniel Defoe. His greatest work is the Leviathan; or, The Matter, Form, and Power of a Commonwealth. His style is clear, manly, and vigorous. He tried to write poetry too. At the advanced age of eighty-five, he wrote a translation of the whole of Homer's Iliad and Odyssey into rhymed English verse, using the same quatrain and the same measure that Dryden employed in his 'Annus Mirabilis.' Two lines are still remembered of this translation: speaking of a child and his mother, he says—

"And like a star upon her bosom lay
His beautiful and shining golden head."

17. JOHN BUNYAN (1628-1688), one of the most popular of our prose-writers, was born at Elstow, in Bedfordshire, in the year 1628— just three years before the birth of Dryden. He served, when a young man, with the Parliamentary forces, and was present at the siege of Leicester. At the Restoration, he was apprehended for preaching, in disobedience to the Conventicle Act, "was had home to prison, and there lay complete twelve years." Here he supported himself and his family by making tagged laces and other small-wares; and here, too, he wrote the immortal Pilgrim's Progress. After his release, he became pastor of the Baptist congregation at Bedford. He had a great power of bringing persons who had quarrelled together again; and he was so popular among those who knew him, that he was generally spoken of as "Bishop Bunyan." On a journey, undertaken to reconcile an estranged father and a rebellious son, he caught a severe cold, and died of fever in London, in the year 1688. Every one has read, or will read, the Pilgrim's Progress; and it may be said, without exaggeration, that to him who has not read the book, a large part of English life and history is dumb and unintelligible. Bunyan has been called the "Spenser of the people," and "the greatest master of allegory that ever lived." His power of imagination is something wonderful; and his simple, homely, and vigorous style makes everything so real, that we seem to be reading a narrative of everyday events and conversations. His vocabulary is not, as Macaulay said, "the vocabulary of the common people;" rather should we say that his English is the English of the Bible and of the best religious writers. His style is, almost everywhere, simple, homely, earnest, and vernacular— without being vulgar. Bunyan's books have, along with Shakespeare and Tyndale's works, been among the chief supports of an idiomatic, nervous, and simple English.

18. JOHN LOCKE (1632-1704), a great English philosopher, was born at Wrington, near Bristol, in the year 1632. He was educated at Oxford; but he took little interest in the Greek and Latin classics, his chief studies lying in medicine and the physical sciences. He became attached to the famous Lord Shaftesbury, under whom he filled several public offices— among others, that of Commissioner of Trade. When Shaftesbury was obliged to flee to Holland, Locke followed him, and spent several years in exile in that country. All his life a very delicate man, he yet, by dint of great care and thoughtfulness, contrived to live to the age of seventy-two. His two most famous works are Some Thoughts concerning Education, and the celebrated Essay on the Human Understanding. The latter, which is his great work, occupied his time and thoughts for eighteen years. In both these books, Locke exhibits the very genius of common-sense. The purpose of education is, in his opinion, not to make learned men, but to maintain "a sound mind in a sound body;" and he begins the education of the future man even from his cradle. In his philosophical writings, he is always simple; but, as he is loose and vacillating in his use of terms, this simplicity is often purchased at the expense of exactness and self-consistency.

CHAPTER VI.

THE FIRST HALF OF THE EIGHTEENTH CENTURY.

1. The Age of Prose.— The eighteenth century was an age of prose in two senses. In the first place, it was a prosaic age; and, in the second place, better prose than poetry was produced by its writers. One remarkable fact may also be noted about the chief prose-writers of this century— and that is, that they were, most of them, not merely able writers, not merely distinguished literary men, but also men of affairs— men well versed in the world and in matters of the highest practical moment, while some were also statesmen holding high office. Thus, in the first half of the century, we find Addison, Swift, and Defoe either holding office or influencing and guiding those who held office; while, in the latter half, we have men like Burke, Hume, and Gibbon, of whom the same, or nearly the same, can be said. The poets, on the contrary, of this eighteenth century, are all of them— with the very slightest exceptions— men who devoted most of their lives to poetry, and had little or nothing to do with practical matters. It may also be noted here that the character of the eighteenth century becomes more and more prosaic as it goes on— less and less under the influence of the spirit of poetry, until, about the close, a great reaction makes itself felt in the persons of Cowper, Chatterton, and Burns, of Crabbe and Wordsworth.

2. The First Half.— The great prose-writers of the first half of the eighteenth century are Addison and Steele, Swift and Defoe. All of these men had some more or less close connection with the rise of journalism in England; and one of them, Defoe, was indeed the founder of the modern newspaper. By far the most powerful intellect of these four was Swift. The greatest poets of the first half of the eighteenth century were Pope, Thomson, Collins, and Gray. Pope towers above all of them by a head and shoulders, because he was much more fertile than any, and because he worked so hard and so untiringly at the labour of the file— at the task of polishing and improving his verses. But the vein of poetry in the three others— and more especially in Collins— was much more pure and genuine than it was in Pope at any time of his life— at any period of his writing. Let us look at each of these writers a little more closely.

3. DANIEL DEFOE (1661-1731), one of the most fertile writers that England ever saw, and one who has been the delight of many generations of readers, was born in the city of London in the year 1661. He was educated to be a Dissenting minister; but he turned from that profession to the pursuit of trade. He attempted several trades,— was a hosier, a hatter, a printer; and he is said also to have been a brick and tile maker. In 1692 he failed in business; but, in no long time after, he paid every one of his creditors to the uttermost farthing. Through all his labours and misfortunes he was always a hard and careful reader,— an omnivorous reader, too, for he was in the habit of reading almost every book that came in his way. He made his first reputation by writing political pamphlets. One of his pamphlets brought him into high favour with King William; another had the effect of placing him in the pillory and lodging him in

prison. But while in Newgate, he did not idle away his time or "languish"; he set to work, wrote hard, and started a newspaper, The Review,— the earliest genuine newspaper England had seen up to his time. This paper he brought out two or three times a-week; and every word of it he wrote himself. He continued to carry it on single-handed for eight years. In 1706, he was made a member of the Commission for bringing about the union between England and Scotland; and his great knowledge of commerce and commercial affairs were of singular value to this Commission. In 1715 he had a dangerous illness, brought on by political excitement; and, on his recovery, he gave up most of his political writing, and took to the composition of stories and romances. Although now a man of fifty-four, he wrote with the vigour and ease of a young man of thirty. His greatest imaginative work was written in 1719— when he was nearly sixty— The Life and Strange Surprising Adventures of Robinson Crusoe, of York, Mariner,... written by Himself. Within six years he had produced twelve works of a similar kind. He is said to have written in all two hundred and fifty books in the course of his lifetime. He died in 1731.

4. His best known— and it is also his greatest— work is Robinson Crusoe; and this book, which every one has read, may be compared with 'Gulliver's Travels,' for the purpose of observing how imaginative effects are produced by different means and in different ways. Another vigorous work of imagination by Defoe is the Journal of the Plague, which appeared in 1722. There are three chief things to be noted regarding Defoe and his writings. These are: first, that Defoe possessed an unparalleled knowledge— a knowledge wider than even Shakespeare's— of the circumstances and details of human life among all sorts, ranks, and conditions of men; secondly, that he gains his wonderful realistic effects by the freest and most copious use of this detailed knowledge in his works of imagination; and thirdly, that he possessed a vocabulary of the most wonderful wealth. His style is strong, homely, and vigorous, but the sentences are long, loose, clumsy, and sometimes ungrammatical. Like Sir Walter Scott, he was too eager to produce large and broad effects to take time to balance his clauses or to polish his sentences. Like Sir Walter Scott, again, he possesses in the highest degree the art of particularising.

5. JONATHAN SWIFT (1667-1745), the greatest prose-writer, in his own kind, of the eighteenth century, and the opposite in most respects— especially in style— of Addison, was born in Dublin in the year 1667. Though born in Ireland, he was of purely English descent— his father belonging to a Yorkshire family, and his mother being a Leicestershire lady. His father died before he was born; and he was educated by the kindness of an uncle. After being at a private school at Kilkenny, he was sent to Trinity College, Dublin, where he was plucked for his degree at his first examination, and, on a second trial, only obtained his B.A. "by special favour." He next came to England, and for eleven years acted as private secretary to Sir William Temple, a retired statesman and ambassador, who lived at Moor Park, near Richmond-on-Thames. In 1692 he paid a visit to Oxford, and there obtained the degree of M.A. In 1700 he went to Ireland with Lord Berkeley as his chaplain, and while in that country was

presented with several livings. He at first attached himself to the Whig party, but stung by this party's neglect of his labours and merits, he joined the Tories, who raised him to the Deanery of St Patrick's Cathedral in Dublin. But, though nominally resident in Dublin, he spent a large part of his time in London. Here he knew and met everybody who was worth knowing, and for some time he was the most imposing figure, and wielded the greatest influence in all the best social, political, and literary circles of the capital. In 1714, on the death of Queen Anne, Swift's hopes of further advancement died out; and he returned to his Deanery, settled in Dublin, and "commenced Irishman for life." A man of strong passions, he usually spent his birthday in reading that chapter of the Book of Job which contains the verse, "Let the day perish in which I was born." He died insane in 1745, and left his fortune to found a lunatic asylum in Dublin. One day, when taking a walk with a friend, he saw a blasted elm, and, pointing to it, he said: "I shall be like that tree, and die first at the top." For the last three years of his life he never spoke one word.

6. Swift has written verse; but it is his prose-works that give him his high and unrivalled place in English literature. His most powerful work, published in 1704, is the Tale of a Tub— a satire on the disputes between the Roman Catholic, Anglican, and Presbyterian Churches. His best known prose-work is the Gulliver's Travels, which appeared in 1726. This work is also a satire; but it is a satire on men and women,— on humanity. "The power of Swift's prose," it has been said by an able critic, "was the terror of his own, and remains the wonder of after times." His style is strong, simple, straightforward; he uses the plainest words and the homeliest English, and every blow tells. Swift's style— as every genuine style does— reflects the author's character. He was an ardent lover and a good hater. Sir Walter Scott describes him as "tall, strong, and well made, dark in complexion, but with bright blue eyes (Pope said they were "as azure as the heavens"), black and bushy eyebrows, aquiline nose, and features which expressed the stern, haughty, and dauntless turn of his mind." He grew savage under the slightest contradiction; and dukes and great lords were obliged to pay court to him. His prose was as trenchant and powerful as were his manners: it has been compared to "cold steel." His own definition of a good style is "proper words in proper places."

7. JOSEPH ADDISON (1672-1719), the most elegant prose-writer— as Pope was the most polished verse-writer— of the eighteenth century, was born at Milston, in Wiltshire, in the year 1672. He was educated at Charterhouse School, in London, where one of his friends and companions was the celebrated Dick Steele— afterwards Sir Richard Steele. He then went to Oxford, where he made a name for himself by his beautiful compositions in Latin verse. In 1695 he addressed a poem to King William; and this poem brought him into notice with the Government of the day. Not long after, he received a pension of £300 a-year, to enable him to travel; and he spent some time in France and Italy. The chief result of this tour was a poem entitled A Letter from Italy to Lord Halifax. In 1704, when Lord Godolphin was in search of a poet who should celebrate in an adequate style the striking victory of Blenheim, Addison was introduced to

him by Lord Halifax. His poem called The Campaign was the result; and one simile in it took and held the attention of all English readers, and of "the town." A violent storm had passed over England; and Addison compared the calm genius of Marlborough, who was as cool and serene amid shot and shell as in a drawing-room or at the dinner-table, to the Angel of the Storm. The lines are these:—

"So when an Angel by divine command
With rising tempests shakes a guilty land,
Such as of late o'er pale Britannia passed,
Calm and serene he drives the furious blast;
And, pleased the Almighty's orders to perform,
Rides in the whirlwind, and directs the storm."

For this poem Addison was rewarded with the post of Commissioner of Appeals. He rose, successively, to be Under Secretary of State; Secretary for Ireland; and, finally, Secretary of State for England— an office which would correspond to that of our present Home Secretary. He married the Countess of Warwick, to whose son he had been tutor; but it was not a happy marriage. Pope says of him in regard to it, that—

"He married discord in a noble wife."

He died at Holland House, Kensington, London, in the year 1719, at the age of forty-seven.

8. But it is not at all as a poet, but as a prose-writer, that Addison is famous in the history of literature. While he was in Ireland, his friend Steele started The Tatler, in 1709; and Addison sent numerous contributions to this little paper. In 1711, Steele began a still more famous paper, which he called The Spectator; and Addison's writings in this morning journal made its reputation. His contributions are distinguishable by being signed with some one of the letters of the name Clio— the Muse of History. A third paper, The Guardian, appeared a few years after; and Addison's contributions to it are designated by a hand ([-]]) at the foot of each. In addition to his numerous prose-writings, Addison brought out the tragedy of Cato in 1713. It was very successful; but it is now neither read nor acted. Some of his hymns, however, are beautiful, and are well known. Such are the hymn beginning, "The spacious firmament on high;" and his version of the 23d Psalm, "The Lord my pasture shall prepare."

9. Addison's prose style is inimitable, easy, graceful, full of humour— full of good humour, delicate, with a sweet and kindly rhythm, and always musical to the ear. He is the most graceful of social satirists; and his genial creation of the character of Sir Roger de Coverley will live for ever. While his work in verse is never more than second-rate, his writings in prose are always first-rate. Dr Johnson said of his prose: "Whoever wishes to attain an English style— familiar but not coarse, and elegant but not ostentatious,— must give his days and nights to the study of Addison." Lord Lytton also remarks: "His style has that nameless urbanity in which we recognise the perfection of manner; courteous, but not

courtier-like; so dignified, yet so kindly; so easy, yet high-bred. It is the most perfect form of English." His style, however, must be acknowledged to want force— to be easy rather than vigorous; and it has not the splendid march of Jeremy Taylor, or the noble power of Savage Landor.

10. RICHARD STEELE (1671-1729), commonly called "Dick Steele," the friend and colleague of Addison, was born in Dublin, but of English parents, in the year 1671. The two friends were educated at Charterhouse and at Oxford together; and they remained friends, with some slight breaks and breezes, to the close of life. Steele was a writer of plays, essays, and pamphlets— for one of which he was expelled from the House of Commons; but his chief fame was earned in connection with the Society Journals, which he founded. He started many— such as Town-Talk, The Tea-Table, Chit-Chat; but only the Tatler and the Spectator rose to success and to fame. The strongest quality in his writing is his pathos: the source of tears is always at his command; and, although himself of a gay and even rollicking temperament, he seems to have preferred this vein. The literary skill of Addison— his happy art in the choosing of words— did not fall to the lot of Steele; but he is more hearty and more human in his description of character. He died in 1729, ten years after the departure of his friend Addison.

11. ALEXANDER POPE (1688-1744), the greatest poet of the eighteenth century, was born in Lombard Street, London, in the year of the Revolution, 1688. His father was a wholesale linendraper, who, having amassed a fortune, retired to Binfield, on the borders of Windsor Forest. In the heart of this beautiful country young Pope's youth was spent. On the death of his father, Pope left Windsor and took up his residence at Twickenham, on the banks of the Thames, where he remained till his death in 1744. His parents being Roman Catholics, it was impossible for young Pope to go either to a public school or to one of the universities; and hence he was educated privately. At the early age of eight, he met with a translation of Homer in verse; and this volume became his companion night and day. At the age of ten, he turned some of the events described in Homer into a play. The poems of Spenser, the poets' poet, were his next favourites; but the writer who made the deepest and most lasting impression upon his mind was Dryden. Little Pope began to write verse very early. He says of himself—
"As yet a child, nor yet a fool to fame,
I lisped in numbers, for the numbers came."

His Ode to Solitude was written at the age of twelve; his Pastorals when he was fifteen. His Essay on Criticism, which was composed in his twentieth year, though not published till 1711, established his reputation as a writer of neat, clear, sparkling, and elegant verse. The Rape of the Lock raised his reputation still higher. Macaulay pronounced it his best poem. De Quincey declared it to be "the most exquisite monument of playful fancy that universal literature offers." Another critic has called it the "perfection of the mock-heroic." Pope's most successful poem— if we measure it by the fame and the money it brought him— was his translation of the Iliad of Homer. A great scholar said of this translation that it was "a very pretty poem, but not Homer." The fact is that Pope did not translate directly from the Greek, but from a French or a Latin version which he kept beside him. Whatever its faults, and however great its deficiency as a representation of the powerful and deep simplicity of the original Greek, no one can deny the charm and finish of its versification, or the rapidity, facility, and melody of the flow of the verse. These qualities make this work unique in English poetry.

12. After finishing the Iliad, Pope undertook a translation of the Odyssey of Homer. This was not so successful; nor was it so well done. In fact, Pope translated only half of it himself; the other half was written by two scholars called Broome and Fenton. His next great poem was the Dunciad,— a satire upon those petty writers, carping critics, and hired defamers who had tried to write down the reputation of Pope's Homeric work. "The composition of the 'Dunciad' revealed to Pope where his true strength lay, in blending personalities with moral reflections."

13. Pope's greatest works were written between 1730 and 1740; and they consist of the Moral Essays, the Essay on Man, and the Epistles and Satires. These poems are full of the finest thoughts, expressed in the most perfect form. Mr Ruskin quotes the couplet—
"Never elated, while one man's oppressed;
Never dejected, whilst another's blessed,"—
as "the most complete, concise, and lofty expression of moral temper existing in English words." The poem of Pope which shows his best and most striking qualities in their most characteristic form, is probably the Epistle to Dr Arbuthnot or Prologue to the Satires. In this poem occur the celebrated lines about Addison— which make a perfect portrait, although it is far from being a true likeness.

His pithy lines and couplets have obtained a permanent place in literature. Thus we have:—
"True wit is nature to advantage dressed,
What oft was thought, but ne'er so well expressed."
"Good-nature and good-sense must ever join.
To err is human, to forgive divine."
"All seems infected that the infected spy,
As all looks yellow to the jaundic'd eye."
"Fear not the anger of the wise to raise;
Those best can bear reproof who merit praise."

The greatest conciseness is visible in his epigrams and in his compliments:—
"A vile encomium doubly ridicules:
There's nothing blackens like the ink of fools."

"And not a vanity is given in vain."

"Would ye be blest? despise low joys, low gains,
Disdain whatever Cornbury disdains,
Be virtuous, and be happy for your pains."

14. Pope is the foremost literary figure of his age and century; and he is also the head of a school. He brought to perfection a style of writing verse which was followed by hundreds of clever writers. Cowper says of him:—

"But Pope— his musical finesse was such,
So nice his ear, so delicate his touch,—
Made poetry a mere mechanic art,
And every warbler has his tune by heart."

Pope was not the poet of nature or of humanity; he was the poet of "the town," and of the Court. He was greatly influenced by the neatness and polish of French verse; and, from his boyhood, his great ambition was to be "a correct poet." He worked and worked, polished and polished, until each idea had received at his hands its very neatest and most epigrammatic expression. In the art of condensed, compact, pointed, and yet harmonious and flowing verse, Pope has no equal. But, as a vehicle for poetry— for the love and sympathy with nature and man which every true poet must feel, Pope's verse is artificial; and its style of expression has now died out. It was one of the chief missions of Wordsworth to drive the Popian second-hand vocabulary out of existence.

15. JAMES THOMSON (1700-1748), the poet of The Seasons, was born at Ednam in Roxburghshire, Scotland, in the year 1700. He was educated at the grammar-school of Jedburgh, and then at the University of Edinburgh. It was intended that he should enter the ministry of the Church of Scotland; but, before his college course was finished, he had given up this idea: poetry proved for him too strong a magnet. While yet a young man, he had written his poem of Winter; and, with that in his pocket, he resolved to try his fortune in London. While walking about the streets, looking at the shops, and gazing at the new wonders of the vast metropolis, his pocket was picked of his pocket-handkerchief and his letters of introduction; and he found himself alone in London— thrown entirely on his own resources. A publisher was, however, in time found for Winter; and the poem slowly rose into appreciation and popularity. This was in 1726. Next year, Summer; two years after, Spring appeared; while Autumn, in 1730, completed the Seasons. The Castle of Indolence— a poem in the Spenserian stanza— appeared in 1748. In the same year he was appointed Surveyor-General of the Leeward Islands, though he never visited the scene of his duty, but had his work done by deputy. He died at Kew in the year 1748.

16. Thomson's place as a poet is high in the second rank. His Seasons have always been popular; and, when Coleridge found a well-thumbed and thickly dog's-eared copy lying on the window-sill of a country inn, he exclaimed "This is true fame!" His Castle of Indolence is, however, a finer piece of poetical work than any of his other writings. The first canto is the best. But the Seasons have been much more widely read; and a modern critic says: "No poet has given the special pleasure which poetry is capable of giving to so large a number of

persons in so large a measure as Thomson." Thomson is very unequal in his style. Sometimes he rises to a great height of inspired expression; at other times he sinks to a dull dead level of pedestrian prose. His power of describing scenery is often very remarkable. Professor Craik says: "There is no other poet who surrounds us with so much of the truth of nature;" and he calls the Castle of Indolence "one of the gems of the language."

17. THOMAS GRAY (1716-1771), the greatest elegiac poet of the century, was born in London in 1716. His father was a "money-scrivener," as it was called; in other words, he was a stock-broker. His mother's brother was an assistant-master at Eton; and at Eton, under the care of this uncle, Gray was brought up. One of his schoolfellows was the famous Horace Walpole. After leaving school, Gray proceeded to Cambridge; but, instead of reading mathematics, he studied classical literature, history, and modern languages, and never took his degree. After some years spent at Cambridge, he entered himself of the Inner Temple; but he never gave much time to the study of law. His father died in 1741; and Gray, soon after, gave up the law and went to live entirely at Cambridge. The first published of his poems was the Ode on a Distant Prospect of Eton College. The Elegy Written in a Country Churchyard was handed about in manuscript before its publication in 1750; and it made his reputation at once. In 1755 the Progress of Poesy was published; and the ode entitled The Bard was begun. In 1768 he was appointed Professor of Modern History at Cambridge; but, though he studied hard, he never lectured. He died at Cambridge, at the age of fifty-four, in the year 1771. Gray was never married. He was said by those who knew him to be the most learned man of his time in Europe. Literature, history, and several sciences— all were thoroughly known to him. He had read everything in the world that was best worth reading; while his knowledge of botany, zoology, and entomology was both wide and exact.

18. Gray's Elegy took him seven years to write; it contains thirty-two stanzas; and Mr Palgrave says "they are perhaps the noblest stanzas in the language." General Wolfe, when sailing down to attack Quebec, recited the Elegy to his officers, and declared, "Now, gentlemen, I would rather be the author of that poem than take Quebec." Lord Byron called the Elegy "the corner-stone of Gray's poetry." Gray ranks with Milton as the most finished workman in English verse; and certainly he spared no pains. Gray said himself that "the style he aimed at was extreme conciseness of expression, yet pure, perspicuous, and musical;" and this style, at which he aimed, he succeeded fully in achieving. One of the finest stanzas in the whole Elegy is the last, which the writer omitted in all the later editions:—

"There scattered oft, the earliest of the year,
By hands unseen, are showers of violets found;
The red-breast loves to build and warble there,
And little footsteps lightly print the ground."

19. WILLIAM COLLINS (1721-1759), one of the truest lyrical poets of the century, was born at Chichester on Christmas-day, 1721. He was educated at Winchester School; afterwards at Queen's, and also at Magdalen College, Oxford. Before he left school he had written a set of poems called Persian Eclogues. He left the university with a reputation for ability and for indolence; went to London "with many projects in his head and little money in his pocket;" and there found a kind and fast friend in Dr Johnson. His Odes appeared in 1747. The volume fell stillborn from the press: not a single copy was sold; no one bought, read, or noticed it. In a fit of furious despair, the unhappy author called in the whole edition and burnt every copy with his own hands. And yet it was, with the single exception of the songs of Burns, the truest poetry that had appeared in the whole of the eighteenth century. A great critic says: "In the little book there was hardly a single false note: there was, above all things, a purity of music, a clarity of style, to which I know of no parallel in English verse from the death of Andrew Marvell to the birth of William Blake." Soon after this great disappointment he went to live at Richmond, where he formed a friendship with Thomson and other poets. In 1749 he wrote the Ode on the Death of Thomson, beginning—

"In yonder grave a Druid lies"—

one of the finest of his poems. Not long after, he was attacked by a disease of the brain, from which he suffered, at intervals, during the remainder of his short life. He died at Chichester in 1759, at the age of thirty-eight.

20. Collins's best poem is the Ode to Evening; his most elaborate, the Ode on the Passions; and his best known, the Ode beginning—

"How sleep the brave, who sink to rest
By all their country's wishes blessed!"

His latest and best critic says of his poems: "His range of flight was perhaps the narrowest, but assuredly the highest, of his generation. He could not be taught singing like a finch, but he struck straight upward for the sun like a lark.... The direct sincerity and purity of their positive and straightforward inspiration will always keep his poems fresh and sweet in the senses of all men. He was a solitary song-bird among many more or less excellent pipers and pianists. He could put more spirit of colour into a single stroke, more breath of music into a single note, than could all the rest of his generation into all the labours of their lives."

CHAPTER VII.

THE SECOND HALF OF THE EIGHTEENTH CENTURY.

1. Prose-Writers.— The four greatest prose-writers of the latter half of the eighteenth century are Johnson, Goldsmith, Burke, and Gibbon. Dr Johnson was the most prominent literary figure in London at this period; and filled in his own time much the same position that Carlyle lately held in literary circles. He wrote on many subjects— but chiefly on literature and morals; and hence he was called "The Great Moralist." Goldsmith stands out clearly as the writer of the most pleasant and easy prose; his pen was ready for any subject; and it has been said of him with perfect truth, that he touched nothing that he did not adorn. Burke was the most eloquent writer of his time, and by far the greatest political thinker that England has ever produced. He is known by an essay he wrote when a very young man— on "The Sublime and Beautiful"; but it is to his speeches and political writings that we must look for his noblest thoughts and most eloquent language. Gibbon is one of the greatest historians and most powerful writers the world has ever seen.

2. SAMUEL JOHNSON (1709-1784), the great essayist and lexicographer, was born at Lichfield in the year 1709. His father was a bookseller; and it was in his father's shop that Johnson acquired his habit of omnivorous reading, or rather devouring of books. The mistress of the dame's school, to which he first went, declared him to be the best scholar she ever had. After a few years at the free grammar-school of Lichfield, and one year at Stourbridge, he went to Pembroke College, Oxford, at the age of nineteen. Here he did not confine himself to the studies of the place, but indulged in a wide range of miscellaneous reading. He was too poor to take a degree, and accordingly left Oxford without graduating. After acting for some time as a bookseller's hack, he married a Mrs Porter of Birmingham— a widow with £800. With this money he opened a boarding-school, or "academy" as he called it; but he had never more than three scholars— the most famous of whom was the celebrated player, David Garrick. In 1737 he went up to London, and for the next quarter of a century struggled for a living by the aid of his pen. During the first ten years of his London life he wrote chiefly for the 'Gentleman's Magazine.' In 1738 his London— a poem in heroic metre— appeared. In 1747 he began his famous Dictionary; it was completed in 1755; and the University of Oxford conferred on him the honorary degree of M.A. In 1749 he wrote another poem— also in heroic metre— the 'Vanity of Human Wishes.' In 1750 he had begun the periodical that raised his fame to its full height— a periodical to which he gave the name of The Rambler. It appeared twice a-week; and Dr Johnson wrote every article in it for two years. In 1759 he published the short novel called Rasselas: it was written to defray the expenses of his mother's funeral; and he wrote it "in the evenings of a week." The year 1762 saw him with a pension from the Government of £300 a-year; and henceforth he was free from heavy hack-work and literary drudgery, and could give himself up to the largest enjoyment of that for which he cared

most— social conversation. He was the best talker of his time; and he knew everybody worth knowing— Burke, Goldsmith, Gibbon, the great painter Sir Joshua Reynolds, and many other able men. In 1764 he founded the "Literary Club," which still exists and meets in London. Oddly enough, although a prolific writer, it is to another person— to Mr James Boswell, who first met him in 1763— that he owes his greatest and most lasting fame. A much larger number of persons read Boswell's Life of Johnson— one of the most entertaining books in all literature— than Johnson's own works. Between the years 1779 and 1781 appeared his last and ablest work, The Lives of the Poets, which were written as prefaces to a collective edition of the English Poets, published by several London booksellers. He died in 1784.

3. Johnson's earlier style was full of Latin words; his later style is more purely English than most of the journalistic writing of the present day. His Rambler is full of "long-tailed words in osity and ation;" but his 'Lives of the Poets' is written in manly, vigorous, and idiomatic English. In verse, he occupies a place between Pope and Goldsmith, and is one of the masters in the "didactic school" of English poetry. His rhythm and periods are swelling and sonorous; and here and there he equals Pope in the terseness and condensation of his language. The following is a fair specimen:—

"Of all the griefs that harass the distressed,
Sure the most bitter is a scornful jest;
Fate never wounds more deep the generous heart,
Than when a blockhead's insult points the dart."

4. OLIVER GOLDSMITH (1728-1774), poet, essayist, historian, and dramatist, was born at Pallas, in the county of Longford, Ireland, in the year 1728. His father was an Irish clergyman, careless, good-hearted, and the original of the famous Dr Primrose, in The Vicar of Wakefield. He was also the original of the "village preacher" in The Deserted Village.

"A man he was to all the country dear,
And passing rich with forty pounds a-year."

Oliver was educated at Trinity College, Dublin; but he left it with no fixed aim. He thought of law, and set off for London, but spent all his money in Dublin. He thought of medicine, and resided two years in Edinburgh. He started for Leyden, in Holland, to continue what he called his medical studies; but he had a thirst to see the world— and so, with a guinea in his pocket, one shirt, and a flute, he set out on his travels through the continent of Europe. At length, on the 1st of February 1756, he landed at Dover, after an absence of two years, without a farthing in his pocket. London reached, he tried many ways of making a living, as assistant to an apothecary, physician, reader for the press, usher in a school, writer in journals. His first work was 'An Inquiry into the State of Polite Learning in Europe,' in 1759; but it appeared without his name. From that date he wrote books of all kinds, poems, and plays. He died in his chambers in Brick Court, Temple, London, in 1774.

5. Goldsmith's best poems are The Traveller and The Deserted Village,— both written in the Popian couplet. His best play is She Stoops to Conquer. His best prose work is The Vicar of Wakefield, "the first genuine novel of domestic life." He also wrote histories of England, of Rome, of Animated Nature. All this was done as professional, nay, almost as hack work; but always in a very pleasant, lively, and readable style. Ease, grace, charm, naturalness, pleasant rhythm, purity of diction— these were the chief characteristics of his writings. "Almost to all things could he turn his hand"— poem, essay, play, story, history, natural science. Even when satirical, he was good-natured; and his Retaliation is the friendliest and pleasantest of satires. In his poetry, his words seem artless, but are indeed delicately chosen with that consummate art which conceals and effaces itself: where he seems most simple and easy, there he has taken most pains and given most labour.

6. EDMUND BURKE (1730-1797) was born at Dublin in the year 1730. He was educated at Trinity College, Dublin; and in 1747 was entered of the Middle Temple, with the purpose of reading for the Bar. In 1766 he was so fortunate as to enter Parliament as member for Wendover, in Buckinghamshire; and he sat in the House of Commons for nearly thirty years. While in Parliament, he worked hard to obtain justice for the colonists of North America, and to avert the separation of them from the mother country; and also to secure good government for India. At the close of his life, it was his intention to take his seat in the House of Peers as Earl Beaconsfield— the title afterwards assumed by Mr Disraeli; but the death of his son, and only child— for whom the honour was really meant and wished— quite broke his heart, and he never carried out his purpose. He died at Beaconsfield in the year 1797. The lines of Goldsmith on Burke, in his poem of "Retaliation," are well known:—

"Here lies our good Edmund, whose genius was such
We scarcely can praise it or blame it too much;
Who, born for the universe, narrowed his mind,
And to party gave up what was meant for mankind;
Who, too deep for his hearers, still went on refining,
And thought of convincing while they thought of dining."

7. Burke's most famous writings are Thoughts on the Cause of the present Discontents, published in 1773; Reflections on the Trench Revolution (1790); and the Letters on a Regicide Peace (1797). His "Thoughts" is perhaps the best of his works in point of style; his "Reflections," are full of passages of the highest and most noble eloquence. Burke has been described by a great critic as "the supreme writer of the century;" and Macaulay says, that "in richness of imagination, he is superior to every orator ancient and modern." In the power of expressing thought in the strongest, fullest, and most vivid manner, he must be classed with Shakespeare and Bacon— and with these writers when at their best.

He indulges in repetitions; but the repetitions are never monotonous; they serve to place the subject in every possible point of view, and to enable us to see all sides of it. He possessed an enormous vocabulary, and had the fullest power over it; "never was a man under whose hands language was more plastic and ductile." He is very fond of metaphor, and is described by an able critic as "the greatest master of metaphor that the world has ever seen."

8. EDWARD GIBBON (1737-1794), the second great prose-writer of the second half of the eighteenth century, was born at Putney, London, in 1737. His father was a wealthy landowner. Young Gibbon was a very sickly child— the only survivor of a delicate family of seven; he was left to pass his time as he pleased, and for the most part to educate himself. But he had the run of several good libraries; and he was an eager and never satiated reader. He was sent to Oxford at the early age of fifteen; and so full was his knowledge in some directions, and so defective in others, that he went there, he tells us himself, "with a stock of knowledge that might have puzzled a doctor, and a degree of ignorance of which a schoolboy would have been ashamed." He was very fond of disputation while at Oxford; and the Dons of the University were astonished to see the pathetic "thin little figure, with a large head, disputing and arguing with the greatest ability." In the course of his reading, he lighted on some French and English books that convinced him for the time of the truth of the Roman Catholic faith; he openly professed his change of belief; and this obliged him to leave the University. His father sent him to Lausanne, and placed him under the care of a Swiss clergyman there, whose arguments were at length successful in bringing him back to a belief in Protestantism. On his return to England in 1758, he lived in his father's house in Hampshire; read largely, as usual; but also joined the Hampshire militia as captain of a company, and the exercises and manoeuvres of his regiment gave him an insight into military matters which was afterwards useful to him when he came to write history. He published his first work in 1761. It was an essay on the study of literature, and was written in French. In 1770 his father died; he came into a fortune, entered Parliament, where he sat for eight years, but never spoke; and, in 1776, he began his history of the Decline and Fall of the Roman Empire. This, by far the greatest of his works, was not completed till 1787, and was published in 1788, on his fifty-first birthday. His account of the completion of the work— it was finished at Lausanne, where he had lived for six years— is full of beauty: "It was on the day, or rather night, of June 27, 1787, between the hours of eleven and twelve, that I wrote the last lines of the last page in a summer-house in my garden. After laying down my pen, I took several turns in a covered walk of acacias, which commands a prospect of the country, the lake, and the mountains. The air was temperate, the sky was serene. The silver orb of the moon was reflected from the waters, and all nature was silent. I will not describe the first emotion of joy on the recovery of my freedom, and perhaps the establishment of my fame. But my pride was soon humbled, and a sober melancholy was spread over my mind by the idea that I had taken an everlasting leave of an old and agreeable companion, and that, whatever might be the future

fate of my history, the life of the historian must be short and precarious." Gibbon died in 1794, about one year before the birth of another great historian, Grote, the author of the 'History of Greece.'

9. Gibbon's book is one of the great historical works of the world. It covers a space of about thirteen centuries, from the reign of Trajan (98), to the fall of the Eastern Empire in 1453; and the amount of reading and study required to write it, must have been almost beyond the power of our conceiving. The skill in arranging and disposing the enormous mass of matter in his history is also unparalleled. His style is said by a critic to be "copious, splendid, elegantly rounded, distinguished by supreme artificial skill." It is remarkable for the proportion of Latin words employed. While some parts of our translation of the Bible contain as much as 96 per cent of pure English words, Gibbon has only 58 per cent: the rest, or 42 per cent, are words of Latin origin. In fact, of all our great English writers, Gibbon stands lowest in his use of pure English words; and the two writers who come nearest him in this respect are Johnson and Swift. The great Greek scholar, Professor Porson, said of Gibbon's style, that "there could not be a better exercise for a schoolboy than to turn a page of it into English."

10. Poets.— The chief poets of the latter half of the eighteenth century belong to a new world, and show very little trace in their writings of eighteenth-century culture, ideas, or prejudices. Most of the best poets who were born in this half of the eighteenth century and began to write in it— such as Crabbe and Wordsworth— are true denizens, in the character of their minds and feelings, of the nineteenth. The greatest poets of the period are Cowper, Crabbe, and Burns; and along with these may be mentioned as little inferior, Chatterton and Blake, two of the most original poets that have appeared in any literature.

11. WILLIAM COWPER (1731-1800), one of the truest, purest, and sweetest of English poets, was born at Great Berkhampstead, in Hertfordshire, in 1731. His father, Dr Cowper, who was a nephew of Lord Chancellor Cowper, was rector of the parish, and chaplain to George II. Young Cowper was educated at Westminster School; and "the great proconsul of India," Warren Hastings, was one of his schoolfellows. After leaving Westminster, he was entered of the Middle Temple, and was also articled to a solicitor. At the age of thirty-one he was appointed one of the Clerks to the House of Lords; but he was so terribly nervous and timid, that he threw up the appointment. He was next appointed Clerk of the Journals— a post which even the shyest man might hold; but, when he found that he would have to appear at the bar of the House of Lords, he went home and attempted to commit suicide. When at school, he had been terribly and persistently bullied; and, about this time, his mind had been somewhat affected by a disappointment in love. The form of his insanity was melancholia; and he had several long and severe attacks of the same disease in the after-course of his life. He had to be placed in the keeping of a physician; and it was only after fifteen months' seclusion that he was able to face the world. Giving up all idea of professional or of public life, he went to live at Huntingdon with the Unwins; and, after the death of Mr Unwin, he removed with Mrs

Unwin to Olney, in Buckinghamshire. Here, in 1773, another attack of melancholia came upon him. In 1779, Cowper joined with Mr Newton, the curate of the parish, in publishing the Olney Hymns, of which he wrote sixty-eight. But it was not till he was past fifty years of age that he betook himself seriously to the writing of poetry. His first volume, which contained Table-Talk, Conversation, Retirement, and other poems in heroic metre, appeared in 1782. His second volume, which included The Task and John Gilpin, was published in 1785. His translation of the Iliad and Odyssey of Homer— a translation into blank verse, which he wrote at the regular rate of forty lines a-day— was published in 1791. Mrs Unwin now had a shock of paralysis; Cowper himself was again seized with mental illness; and from 1791 till his death in 1800, his condition was one of extreme misery, depression, and despair. He thought himself an outcast from the mercy of God. "I seem to myself," he wrote to a friend, "to be scrambling always in the dark, among rocks and precipices, without a guide, but with an enemy ever at my heels, prepared to push me headlong." The cloud never lifted; gloom and dejection enshrouded all his later years; a pension of £300 a-year from George III. brought him no pleasure; and he died insane, at East Dereham, in Norfolk, in the year 1800. In the poem of The Castaway he compares himself to a drowning sailor:—

"No voice divine the storm allayed,
  No light propitious shone,
When, far from all effectual aid,
  We perished— each alone—
But I beneath a rougher sea,
And whelmed in blacker gulfs than he."

12. His greatest work is The Task; and the best poem in it is probably "The Winter Evening." His best-known poem is John Gilpin, which, like "The Task," he wrote at the request of his friend, Lady Austen. His most powerful poem is The Castaway. He always writes in clear, crisp, pleasant, and manly English. He himself says, in a letter to a friend: "Perspicuity is always more than half the battle... A meaning that does not stare you in the face is as bad as no meaning;" and this direction he himself always carried out. Cowper's poems mark a new era in poetry; his style is new, and his ideas are new. He is no follower of Pope; Southey compared Pope and Cowper as "formal gardens in comparison with woodland scenery." He is always original, always true— true to his own feeling, and true to the object he is describing. "My descriptions," he writes of "The Task," "are all from nature; not one of them second-handed. My delineations of the heart are from my own experience." Everywhere in his poems we find a genuine love of nature; humour and pathos in his description of persons; and a purity and honesty of style that have never been surpassed. Many of his well-put lines have passed into our common stock of everyday quotations. Such are—
    "God made the country, and man made the town."

"Variety's the very spice of life
That gives it all its flavour."

    "The heart
May give a useful lesson to the head,
And Learning wiser grow without his books."

"Beware of desperate steps. The darkest day,
Live till to-morrow, will have passed away."

13. GEORGE CRABBE (1754-1832), the poet of the poor, was born at Aldborough, in Suffolk, on Christmas Eve of the year 1754. He stands thus midway between Goldsmith and Wordsworth— midway between the old and the new school of poetry. His father was salt-master— or collector of salt duties— at the little seaport. After being taught a little at several schools, it was agreed that George should be made a surgeon. He was accordingly apprenticed; but he was fonder of writing verses than of attending cases. His memory for poetry was astonishing; he had begun to write verses at the age of fourteen; and he filled the drawers of the surgery with his poetical attempts. After a time he set up for himself in practice at Aldborough; but most of his patients were poor people and poor relations, who paid him neither for his physic nor his advice. In 1779 he resolved "to go to London and venture all." Accordingly, he took a berth on board of a sailing-packet, carrying with him a little money and a number of manuscript poems. But nothing succeeded with him; he was reduced to his last eightpence. In this strait, he wrote to the great statesman, Edmund Burke; and, while the answer was coming, he walked all night up and down Westminster Bridge. Burke took him in to his own house and found a publisher for his poems.

14. In 1781 The Library appeared; and in the same year Crabbe entered the Church. In 1783 he published The Village— a poem which Dr Johnson revised for him. This work won for him an established reputation; but, for twenty-four years after, Crabbe gave himself up entirely to the care of his parish, and published only one poem— The Newspaper. In 1807 appeared The Parish Register; in 1810, The Borough; in 1812, Tales in Verse; and, in 1819, his last poetical work, Tales of the Hall. From this time, till his death in 1832— thirteen years after— he produced no other poem. Personally, he was one of the noblest and kindest of men; he was known as "the gentleman with the sour name and the sweet countenance;" and he spent most of his income on the wants of others.

15. Crabbe's poetical work forms a prominent landmark in English literature. His style is the style of the eighteenth century— with a strong admixture of his own; his way of thinking, and the objects he selects for description, belong to the nineteenth. While Pope depicted "the town," politics, and abstract moralities, Crabbe describes the country and the country poor, social matters, real life— the lowest and poorest life, and more especially, the intense misery of the village population of his time in the eastern counties—

"the wild amphibious race
With sullen woe displayed in every face."

He does not paint the lot of the poor with the rose-coloured tints used by Goldsmith; he boldly denies the existence of such a village as Auburn; he groups such places with Eden, and says—

"Auburn and Eden can be found no more;"

he shows the gloomy, hard, despairing side of English country life. He has been called a "Pope in worsted stockings," and "the Hogarth, of song." Byron describes him as

"Nature's sternest painter, yet the best."

Now and then his style is flat, and even coarse; but there is everywhere a genuine power of strong and bold painting. He is also an excellent master of easy dialogue.

All of his poems are written in the Popian couplet of two ten-syllabled lines.

16. ROBERT BURNS (1759-1796), the greatest poet of Scotland, was born in Ayrshire, two miles from the town of Ayr, in 1759. The only education he received from his father was the schooling of a few months; but the family were fond of reading, and Robert was the most enthusiastic reader of them all. Every spare moment he could find— and they were not many— he gave to reading; he sat at meals "with a book in one hand and a spoon in the other;" and in this way he read most of the great English poets and prose-writers. This was an excellent education— one a great deal better than most people receive; and some of our greatest men have had no better. But, up to the age of sixteen, he had to toil on his father's farm from early morning till late at night. In the intervals of his work he contrived, by dint of thrift and industry, to learn French, mathematics, and a little Latin. On the death of his father, he took a small farm, but did not succeed. He was on the point of embarking for Jamaica, where a post had been found for him, when the news of the successful sale of a small volume of his poems reached him; and he at once changed his mind, and gave up all idea of emigrating. His friends obtained for him a post as exciseman, in which his duty was to gauge the quantity and quality of ardent spirits— a post full of dangers to a man of his excitable and emotional temperament. He went a great deal into what was called society, formed the acquaintance of many boon companions, acquired habits of intemperance that he could not shake off, and died at Dumfries in 1796, in his thirty-seventh year.

17. His best poems are lyrical, and he is himself one of the foremost lyrical poets in the world. His songs have probably been more sung, and in more parts of the globe, than the songs of any other writer that ever lived. They are of every kind— songs of love, war, mirth, sorrow, labour, and social gatherings. Professor Craik says: "One characteristic that belongs to whatever Burns has written is that, of its kind and in its own way, it is a perfect production. His poetry is, throughout, real emotion melodiously uttered, instinct with passion, but not less so with power of thought,— full of light as well as of fire." Most of his poems are written in the North-English, or Lowland-Scottish, dialect. The most elevated of his poems is The Vision, in which he relates how the Scottish

Muse found him at the plough, and crowned him with a wreath of holly. One of his longest, as well as finest poems, is The Cottar's Saturday Night, which is written in the Spenserian stanza. Perhaps his most pathetic poem is that entitled To Mary in Heaven. It is of a singular eloquence, elevation, and sweetness. The first verse runs thus—

"Thou lingering star, with lessening ray,
  That lov'st to greet the early morn,
Again thou usher'st in the day
  My Mary from my soul was torn.
O Mary! dear departed shade!
  Where is thy place of blissful rest?
See'st thou thy lover lowly laid?
  Hear'st thou the groans that rend his breast?"

He is, as his latest critic says, "the poet of homely human nature;" and his genius shows the beautiful elements in this homeliness; and that what is homely need not therefore be dull and prosaic.

18. THOMAS CHATTERTON and WILLIAM BLAKE are two minor poets, of whom little is known and less said, but whose work is of the most poetical and genuine kind. —Chatterton was born at Bristol in the year 1752. He was the son of a schoolmaster, who died before he was born. He was educated at Colston's Blue-Coat School in Bristol; and, while at school, read his way steadily through every book in three circulating libraries. He began to write verses at the age of fifteen, and in two years had produced a large number of poems— some of them of the highest value. In 1770, he came up to London, with something under five pounds in his pocket, and his mind made up to try his fortune as a literary man, resolved, though he was only a boy of seventeen, to live by literature or to die. Accordingly, he set to work and wrote every kind of productions— poems, essays, stories, political articles, songs for public singers; and all the time he was half starving. A loaf of bread lasted him a week; and it was "bought stale to make it last longer." He had made a friend of the Lord Mayor, Beckford; but before he had time to hold out a hand to the struggling boy, Beckford died. The struggle became harder and harder— more and more hopeless; his neighbours offered a little help— a small coin or a meal— he rejected all; and at length, on the evening of the 24th August 1770, he went up to his garret, locked himself in, tore up all his manuscripts, took poison, and died. He was only seventeen.

19. Wordsworth and Coleridge spoke with awe of his genius; Keats dedicated one of his poems to his memory; and Coleridge copied some of his rhythms. One of his best poems is the Minstrel's Roundelay—

"O sing unto my roundelay,
  O drop the briny tear with me,
Dance no more on holy-day,

Like a running river be.
  My love is dead,
    Gone to his death-bed
All under the willow-tree.

"Black his hair as the winter night,
  White his skin as the summer snow,
Red his face as the morning light,
  Cold he lies in the grave below.
    My love is dead,
  Gone to his death-bed
All under the willow-tree."

20. WILLIAM BLAKE (1757-1827), one of the most original poets that ever lived, was born in London in the year 1757. He was brought up as an engraver; worked steadily at his business, and did a great deal of beautiful work in that capacity. He in fact illustrated his own poems— each page being set in a fantastic design of his own invention, which he himself engraved. He was also his own printer and publisher. The first volume of his poems was published in 1783; the Songs of Innocence, probably his best, appeared in 1787. He died in Fountain Court, Strand, London, in the year 1827.

21. His latest critic says of Blake: "His detachment from the ordinary currents of practical thought left to his mind an unspoiled and delightful simplicity which has perhaps never been matched in English poetry." Simplicity— the perfect simplicity of a child— beautiful simplicity— simple and childlike beauty,— such is the chief note of the poetry of Blake. "Where he is successful, his work has the fresh perfume and perfect grace of a flower." The most remarkable point about Blake is that, while living in an age when the poetry of Pope— and that alone— was everywhere paramount, his poems show not the smallest trace of Pope's influence, but are absolutely original. His work, in fact, seems to be the first bright streak of the golden dawn that heralded the approach of the full and splendid daylight of the poetry of Wordsworth and Coleridge, of Shelley and Byron. His best-known poems are those from the 'Songs of Innocence'— such as Piping down the valleys wild; The Lamb; The Tiger, and others. Perhaps the most remarkable element in Blake's poetry is the sweetness and naturalness of the rhythm. It seems careless, but it is always beautiful; it grows, it is not made; it is like a wild field-flower thrown up by Nature in a pleasant green field. Such are the rhythms in the poem entitled Night:—

"The sun descending in the west,
The evening star does shine;
The birds are silent in their nest,
And I must seek for mine.
The moon, like a flower

In heaven's high bower,
With silent delight
Sits and smiles on the night.

"Farewell, green fields and happy grove,
Where flocks have ta'en delight;
Where lambs have nibbled, silent move
The feet of angels bright:
Unseen they pour blessing,
And joy without ceasing,
On each bud and blossom,
On each sleeping bosom."

CHAPTER VIII.

THE FIRST HALF OF THE NINETEENTH CENTURY.

1. New Ideas.— The end of the eighteenth and the beginning of the nineteenth century are alike remarkable for the new powers, new ideas, and new life thrown into society. The coming up of a high flood-tide of new forces seems to coincide with the beginning of the French Revolution in 1789, when the overthrow of the Bastille marked the downfall of the old ways of thinking and acting, and announced to the world of Europe and America that the old régime— the ancient mode of governing— was over. Wordsworth, then a lad of nineteen, was excited by the event almost beyond the bounds of self-control. He says in his "Excursion"—

"Bliss was it in that dawn to be alive,
But to be young was very Heaven!"

It was, indeed, the dawn of a new day for the peoples of Europe. The ideas of freedom and equality— of respect for man as man— were thrown into popular form by France; they became living powers in Europe; and in England they animated and inspired the best minds of the time— Burns, Coleridge, Wordsworth, Shelley, and Byron. Along with this high tide of hope and emotion, there was such an outburst of talent and genius in every kind of human endeavour in England, as was never seen before except in the Elizabethan period. Great events produced great powers; and great powers in their turn brought about great events. The war with America, the long struggle with Napoleon, the new political ideas, great victories by sea and land,— all these were to be found in the beginning of the nineteenth century. The English race produced great men in numbers— almost, it might be said, in groups. We had great leaders, like Nelson and Wellington; brilliant generals, like Sir Charles Napier and Sir John Moore; great statesmen, like Fox and Pitt, like Washington and Franklin; great engineers, like Stephenson and Brunel; and great poets, like Wordsworth and Byron. And as regards literature, an able critic remarks: "We have recovered in this century the Elizabethan magic and passion, a more than Elizabethan sense of the beauty and complexity of nature, the Elizabethan music of language."

2. Great Poets.— The greatest poets of the first half of the nineteenth century may be best arranged in groups. There were Wordsworth, Coleridge, and Southey— commonly, but unnecessarily, described as the Lake Poets. In their poetic thought and expression they had little in common; and the fact that two of them lived most of their lives in the Lake country, is not a sufficient justification for the use of the term. There were Scott and Campbell— both of them Scotchmen. There were Byron and Shelley— both Englishmen, both brought up at the great public schools and the universities, but both carried away by the influence of the new revolutionary ideas. Lastly, there were Moore, an Irishman, and young Keats, the splendid promise of whose youth went out in an

early death. Let us learn a little more about each, and in the order of the dates of their birth.

3. WILLIAM WORDSWORTH (1770-1850) was born at Cockermouth, a town in Cumberland, which stands at the confluence of the Cocker and the Derwent. His father, John Wordsworth, was law agent to Sir James Lowther, who afterwards became Earl of Lonsdale. William was a boy of a stiff, moody, and violent temper; and as his mother died when he was a very little boy, and his father when he was fourteen, he grew up with very little care from his parents and guardians. He was sent to school at Hawkshead, in the Vale of Esthwaite, in Lancashire; and, at the age of seventeen, proceeded to St John's College, Cambridge. After taking his degree of B.A. in 1791, he resided for a year in France. He took sides with one of the parties in the Reign of Terror, and left the country only in time to save his head. He was designed by his uncles for the Church; but a friend, Raisley Calvert, dying, left him £900; and he now resolved to live a plain and frugal life, to join no profession, but to give himself wholly up to the writing of poetry. In 1798, he published, along with his friend, S. T. Coleridge, the Lyrical Ballads. The only work of Coleridge's in this volume was the "Ancient Mariner." In 1802 he married Mary Hutchinson, of whom he speaks in the well-known lines—

"Her eyes as stars of Twilight fair,
Like Twilight's, too, her dusky hair;
But all things else about her drawn
From May-time and the cheerful dawn."

He obtained the post of Distributor of Stamps for the county of Westmoreland; and, after the death of Southey, he was created Poet-Laureate by the Queen. —He settled with his wife in the Lake country; and, in 1813, took up his abode at Rydal Mount, where he lived till his death in 1850. He died on the 23d of April— the death-day of Shakespeare.

4. His longest works are the Excursion and the Prelude— both being parts of a longer and greater work which he intended to write on the growth of his own mind. His best poems are his shorter pieces, such as the poems on Lucy, The Cuckoo, the Ode to Duty, the Intimations of Immortality, and several of his Sonnets. He says of his own poetry that his purpose in writing it was "to console the afflicted; to add sunshine to daylight by making the happy happier; to teach the young and the gracious of every age to see, to think, and feel, and therefore to become more actively and securely virtuous." His poetical work is the noble landmark of a great transition— both in thought and in style. He drew aside poetry from questions and interests of mere society and the town to the scenes of Nature and the deepest feelings of man as man. In style, he refused to employ the old artificial vocabulary which Pope and his followers revelled in; he used the simplest words he could find; and, when he hits the mark in his simplest form of expression, his style is as forcible as it is true. He says of his own verse—

"The moving accident is not my trade,
To freeze the blood I have no ready arts;
'Tis my delight, alone, in summer shade,
 To pipe a simple song for thinking hearts."

If one were asked what four lines of his poetry best convey the feeling of the whole, the reply must be that these are to be found in his "Song at the Feast of Brougham Castle,"— lines written about "the good Lord Clifford."

"Love had he found in huts where poor men lie,
His daily teachers had been woods and rills,—
The silence that is in the starry sky,
The sleep that is among the lonely hills."

5. WALTER SCOTT (1771-1832), poet and novelist, the son of a Scotch attorney (called in Edinburgh a W.S. or Writer to H.M.'s Signet), was born there in the year 1771. He was educated at the High School, and then at the College— now called the University— of Edinburgh. In 1792 he was called to the Scottish Bar, or became an "advocate." During his boyhood, he had had several illnesses, one of which left him lame for life. Through those long periods of sickness and of convalescence, he read Percy's 'Reliques of Ancient Poetry,' and almost all the romances, old plays, and epic poems that have been published in the English language. This gave his mind and imagination a set which they never lost all through life.

6. His first publications were translations of German poems. In the year 1805, however, an original poem, the Lay of the Last Minstrel, appeared; and Scott became at one bound the foremost poet of the day. Marmion, the Lady of the Lake, and other poems, followed with great rapidity. But, in 1814, Scott took it into his head that his poetical vein was worked out; the star of Byron was rising upon the literary horizon; and he now gave himself up to novel-writing. His first novel, Waverley, appeared anonymously in 1814. Guy Mannering, Old Mortality, Rob Roy, and others, quickly followed; and, though the secret of the authorship was well kept both by printer and publisher, Walter Scott was generally believed to be the writer of these works, and he was frequently spoken of as "the Great Unknown." He was made a baronet by George IV. in 1820.

7. His expenses in building Abbotsford, and his desire to acquire land, induced him to go into partnership with Ballantyne, his printer, and with Constable, his publisher. Both firms failed in the dark year of 1826; and Scott found himself unexpectedly liable for the large sum of £147,000. Such a load of debt would have utterly crushed most men; but Scott stood clear and undaunted in front of it. "Gentlemen," he said to his creditors, "time and I against any two. Let me take this good ally into my company, and I believe I shall be able to pay you every farthing." He left his beautiful country house at Abbotsford; he gave up all his country pleasures; he surrendered all his property to his creditors; he

took a small house in Edinburgh; and, in the short space of five years, he had paid off £130,000. But the task was too terrible; the pace had been too hard; and he was struck down by paralysis. But even this disaster did not daunt him. Again he went to work, and again he had a paralytic stroke. At last, however, he was obliged to give up; the Government of the day placed a royal frigate at his disposal; he went to Italy; but his health had utterly broken down, he felt he could get no good from the air of the south, and he turned his face towards home to die. He breathed his last breath at Abbotsford, in sight of his beloved Tweed, with his family around him, on the 21st of September 1832.

8. His poetry is the poetry of action. In imaginative power he ranks below no other poet, except Homer and Shakespeare. He delighted in war, in its movement, its pageantry, and its events; and, though lame, he was quartermaster of a volunteer corps of cavalry. On one occasion he rode to muster one hundred miles in twenty-four hours, composing verses by the way. Much of "Marmion" was composed on horseback. "I had many a grand gallop," he says, "when I was thinking of 'Marmion.'" His two chief powers in verse are his narrative and his pictorial power. His boyhood was passed in the Borderland of Scotland— "a district in which every field has its battle and every rivulet its song;" and he was at home in every part of the Highlands and the Lowlands, the Islands and the Borders, of his native country. But, both in his novels and his poems, he was a painter of action rather than of character.

9. His prose works are now much more read than his poems; but both are full of life, power, literary skill, knowledge of men and women, and strong sympathy with all past ages. He wrote so fast that his sentences are often loose and ungrammatical; but they are never unidiomatic or stiff. The rush of a strong and large life goes through them, and carries the reader along, forgetful of all minor blemishes. His best novels are Old Mortality and Kenilworth; his greatest romance is Ivanhoe.

10. SAMUEL TAYLOR COLERIDGE (1772-1834), a true poet, and a writer of noble prose, was born at Ottery St Mary, in Devonshire, in 1772. His father, who was vicar of the parish, and master of the grammar-school, died when the boy was only nine years of age. He was educated at Christ's Hospital, in London, where his most famous schoolfellow was Charles Lamb; and from there he went to Jesus College, Cambridge. In 1793 he had fallen into debt at College; and, in despair, left Cambridge, and enlisted in the 15th Light Dragoons, under the name of Silas Tomkins Comberbatch. He was quickly discovered, and his discharge soon obtained. While on a visit to his friend Robert Southey, at Bristol, the plan of emigrating to the banks of the Susquehanna, in Pennsylvania, was entered on; but, when all the friends and fellow-emigrants were ready to start, it was discovered that no one of them had any money. —Coleridge finally became a literary man and journalist. His real power, however, lay in poetry; but by poetry he could not make a living. His first volume of poems was published at Bristol, in the year 1796; but it was not till 1798 that the Rime of the Ancient Mariner appeared in the 'Lyrical Ballads.' His next greatest poem, Christabel, though written in 1797, was not published till the

year 1816. His other best poems are Love; Dejection—an Ode; and some of his shorter pieces. His best poetry was written about the close of the century: "Coleridge," said Wordsworth, "was in blossom from 1796 to 1800." —As a critic and prose-writer, he is one of the greatest men of his time. His best works in prose are The Friend and the Aids to Reflection. He died at Highgate, near London, in the year 1834.

11. His style, both in prose and in verse, marks the beginning of the modern era. His prose style is noble, elaborate, eloquent, and full of subtle and involved thought; his style in verse is always musical, and abounds in rhythms of the most startling and novel— yet always genuine— kind. Christabel is the poem that is most full of these fine musical rhythms.

12. ROBERT SOUTHEY (1774-1843), poet, reviewer, historian, but, above all, man of letters,— the friend of Coleridge and Wordsworth,— was born at Bristol in 1774. He was educated at Westminster School and at Balliol College, Oxford. After his marriage with Miss Edith Fricker— a sister of Sara, the wife of Coleridge— he settled at Greta Hall, near Keswick, in 1803; and resided there until his death in 1843. In 1813 he was created Poet-Laureate by George III. — He was the most indefatigable of writers. He wrote poetry before breakfast; history between breakfast and dinner; reviews between dinner and supper; and, even when taking a constitutional, he had always a book in his hand, and walked along the road reading. He began to write and to publish at the age of nineteen; he never ceased writing till the year 1837, when his brain softened from the effects of perpetual labour.

13. Southey wrote a great deal of verse, but much more prose. His prose works amount to more than one hundred volumes; but his poetry, such as it is, will probably live longer than his prose. His best-known poems are Joan of Arc, written when he was nineteen; Thalaba the Destroyer, a poem in irregular and unrhymed verse; The Curse of Kehama, in verse rhymed, but irregular; and Roderick, the last of the Goths, written in blank verse. He will, however, always be best remembered by his shorter pieces, such as The Holly Tree, Stanzas written in My Library, and others. —His most famous prose work is the Life of Nelson. His prose style is always firm, clear, compact, and sensible.

14. THOMAS CAMPBELL (1777-1844), a noble poet and brilliant reviewer, was born in Glasgow in the year 1777. He was educated at the High School and the University of Glasgow. At the age of twenty-two, he published his Pleasures of Hope, which at once gave him a place high among the poets of the day. In 1803 he removed to London, and followed literature as his profession; and, in 1806, he received a pension of £200 a-year from the Government, which enabled him to devote the whole of his time to his favourite study of poetry. His best long poem is the Gertrude of Wyoming, a tale written in the Spenserian stanza, which he handles with great ease and power. But he is best known, and will be longest remembered, for his short lyrics— which glow with passionate and fiery eloquence— such as The Battle of the Baltic, Ye Mariners of England, Hohenlinden, and others. He was twice Lord Rector of the University of

Glasgow. He died at Boulogne in 1844, and was buried in Poets' Corner, Westminster Abbey.

15. THOMAS MOORE (1779-1852), poet, biographer, and historian— but most of all poet— was born in Dublin in the year 1779. He began to print verses at the age of thirteen, and may be said, like Pope, to have "lisped in numbers, for the numbers came." He came to London in 1799, and was quickly received into fashionable society. In 1803 he was made Admiralty Registrar at Bermuda; but he soon gave up the post, leaving a deputy in his place, who, some years after, embezzled the Government funds, and brought financial ruin upon Moore. The poet's friends offered to help him out of his money difficulties; but he most honourably declined all such help, and, like Sir W. Scott, resolved to clear off all claims against him by the aid of his pen alone. For the next twenty years of his life he laboured incessantly; and volumes of poetry, history, and biography came steadily from his pen. His best poems are his Irish Melodies, some fifteen or sixteen of which are perfect and imperishable; and it is as a writer of songs that Moore will live in the literature of this country. He boasted, and with truth, that it was he who awakened for this century the long-silent harp of his native land—

"Dear Harp of my Country! in darkness I found thee,
  The cold chain of silence had hung o'er thee long,
When proudly, my own Island Harp, I unbound thee,
  And gave all thy chords to light, freedom, and song."

His best long poem is Lalla Rookh. —His prose works are little read nowadays. The chief among them are his Life of Sheridan, and his Life of Lord Byron. —He died at Sloperton, in Wiltshire, in 1852, two years after the death of Wordsworth.

16. GEORGE GORDON, LORD BYRON (1788-1824), a great English poet, was born in London in the year 1788. He was the only child of a reckless and unprincipled father and a passionate mother. He was educated at Harrow School, and afterwards at Trinity College, Cambridge. His first volume— Hours of Idleness— was published in 1807, before he was nineteen. A critique of this juvenile work which appeared in the 'Edinburgh Review' stung him to passion; and he produced a very vigorous poetical reply in English Bards and Scotch Reviewers. After the publication of this book, Byron travelled in Germany, Spain, Greece, and Turkey for two years; and the first two cantos of the poem entitled Childe Harold's Pilgrimage were the outcome of these travels. This poem at once placed him at the head of English poets; "he woke one morning," he said, "and found himself famous." He was married in the year 1815, but left his wife in the following year; left his native country also, never to return. First of all he settled at Geneva, where he made the acquaintance of the poet Shelley, and where he wrote, among other poems, the third canto of Childe Harold and the Prisoner of Chillon. In 1817 he removed to Venice, where he composed the fourth canto of Childe Harold and the Lament of Tasso; his next resting-place was Ravenna, where he wrote several plays. Pisa saw him next; and at this place

he spent a great deal of his time in close intimacy with Shelley. In 1821 the Greek nation rose in revolt against the cruelties and oppression of the Turkish rule; and Byron's sympathies were strongly enlisted on the side of the Greeks. He helped the struggling little country with contributions of money; and, in 1823, sailed from Geneva to take a personal share in the war of liberation. He died, however, of fever, at Missolonghi, on the 19th of April 1824, at the age of thirty-six.

17. His best-known work is Childe Harold, which is written in the Spenserian stanza. His plays, the best of which are Manfred and Sardanap[-a]lus, are written in blank verse. —His style is remarkable for its strength and elasticity, for its immensely powerful sweep, tireless energy, and brilliant illustrations.

18. PERCY BYSSHE SHELLEY (1792-1822),— who has, like Spenser, been called "the poet's poet,"— was born at Field Place, near Horsham, in Sussex, in the year 1792. He was educated at Eton, and then at University College, Oxford. A shy, diffident, retiring boy, with sweet, gentle looks and manners— like those of a girl— but with a spirit of the greatest fearlessness and the noblest independence, he took little share in the sports and pursuits of his schoolfellows. Obliged to leave Oxford, in consequence of having written a tract of which the authorities did not approve, he married at the very early age of nineteen. The young lady whom he married died in 1816; and he soon after married Mary, daughter of William Godwin, the eminent author of 'Political Justice.' In 1818 he left England for Italy,— like his friend, Lord Byron, for ever. It was at Naples, Leghorn, and Pisa that he chiefly resided. In 1822 he bought a little boat— "a perfect plaything for the summer," he calls it; and he used often to make short voyages in it, and wrote many of his poems on these occasions. When Leigh Hunt was lying ill at Leghorn, Shelley and his friend Williams resolved on a coasting trip to that city. They reached Leghorn in safety; but, on the return journey, the boat sank in a sudden squall. Captain Roberts was watching the vessel with his glass from the top of the Leghorn lighthouse, as it crossed the Bay of Spezzia: a black cloud arose; a storm came down; the vessels sailing with Shelley's boat were wrapped in darkness; the cloud passed; the sun shone out, and all was clear again; the larger vessels rode on; but Shelley's boat had disappeared. The poet's body was cast on shore, but the quarantine laws of Italy required that everything thrown up on the coast should be burned: no representations could alter the law; and Shelley's ashes were placed in a box and buried in the Protestant cemetery at Rome.

19. Shelley's best long poem is the Adonaïs, an elegy on the death of John Keats. It is written in the Spenserian stanza. But this true poet will be best remembered by his short lyrical poems, such as The Cloud, Ode to a Skylark, Ode to the West Wind, Stanzas written in Dejection, and others. —Shelley has been called "the poet's poet," because his style is so thoroughly transfused by pure imagination. He has also been called "the master-singer of our modern race and age; for his thoughts, his words, and his deeds all sang together." He is probably the greatest lyric poet of this century.

20. JOHN KEATS (1795-1821), one of our truest poets, was born in Moorfields, London, in the year 1795. He was educated at a private school at Enfield. His desire for the pleasures of the intellect and the imagination showed itself very early at school; and he spent many a half-holiday in writing translations from the Roman and the French poets. On leaving school, he was apprenticed to a surgeon at Edmonton— the scene of one of John Gilpin's adventures; but, in 1817, he gave up the practice of surgery, devoted himself entirely to poetry, and brought out his first volume. In 1818 appeared his Endymion. The 'Quarterly Review' handled it without mercy. Keats's health gave way; the seeds of consumption were in his frame; and he was ordered to Italy in 1820, as the last chance of saving his life. But it was too late. The air of Italy could not restore him. He settled at Rome with his friend Severn; but, in spite of all the care, thought, devotion, and watching of his friend, he died in 1821, at the age of twenty-five. He was buried in the Protestant cemetery at Rome; and the inscription on his tomb, composed by himself, is, "Here lies one whose name was writ in water."

21. His greatest poem is Hyperion, written, in blank verse, on the overthrow of the "early gods" of Greece. But he will most probably be best remembered by his marvellous odes, such as the Ode to a Nightingale, Ode on a Grecian Urn, To Autumn, and others. His style is clear, sensuous, and beautiful; and he has added to our literature lines that will always live. Such are the following:—

"A thing of beauty is a joy for ever."
"Silent, upon a peak in Darien."
"Then felt I like some watcher of the skies
When a new planet swims into his ken."

"Perhaps the self-same song that found a path
Through the sad heart of Ruth, when, sick for home,
She stood in tears amid the alien corn."

22. Prose-Writers.— We have now to consider the greatest prose-writers of the first half of the nineteenth century. First comes Walter Scott, one of the greatest novelists that ever lived, and who won the name of "The Wizard of the North" from the marvellous power he possessed of enchaining the attention and fascinating the minds of his readers. Two other great writers of prose were Charles Lamb and Walter Savage Landor, each in styles essentially different. Jane Austen, a young English lady, has become a classic in prose, because her work is true and perfect within its own sphere. De Quincey is perhaps the writer of the most ornate and elaborate English prose of this period. Thomas Carlyle, a great Scotsman, with a style of overwhelming power, but of occasional grotesqueness, like a great prophet and teacher of the nation, compelled statesmen and philanthropists to think, while he also gained for himself a high place in the rank of historians. Macaulay, also of Scottish descent, was one of the greatest essayists and ablest writers on history that Great Britain has produced. A short

survey of each of these great men may be useful. Scott has been already treated of.

23. CHARLES LAMB (1775-1834), a perfect English essayist, was born in the Inner Temple, in London, in the year 1775. His father was clerk to a barrister of that Inn of Court. Charles was educated at Christ's Hospital, where his most famous schoolfellow was S. T. Coleridge. Brought up in the very heart of London, he had always a strong feeling for the greatness of the metropolis of the world. "I often shed tears," he said, "in the motley Strand, for fulness of joy at so much life." He was, indeed, a thorough Cockney and lover of London, as were also Chaucer, Spenser, Milton, and Lamb's friend Leigh Hunt. Entering the India House as a clerk in the year 1792, he remained there thirty-three years; and it was one of his odd sayings that, if any one wanted to see his "works," he would find them on the shelves of the India House. —He is greatest as a writer of prose; and his prose is, in its way, unequalled for sweetness, grace, humour, and quaint terms, among the writings of this century. His best prose work is the Essays of Elia, which show on every page the most whimsical and humorous subtleties, a quick play of intellect, and a deep sympathy with the sorrows and the joys of men. Very little verse came from his pen. "Charles Lamb's nosegay of verse," says Professor Dowden, "may be held by the small hand of a maiden, and there is not in it one flaunting flower." Perhaps the best of his poems are the short pieces entitled Hester and The Old Familiar Faces. —He retired from the India House, on a pension, in 1825, and died at Edmonton, near London, in 1834. His character was as sweet and refined as his style; Wordsworth spoke of him as "Lamb the frolic and the gentle;" and these and other fine qualities endeared him to a large circle of friends.

24. WALTER SAVAGE LANDOR (1775-1864), the greatest prose-writer in his own style of the nineteenth century, was born at Ipsley Court, in Warwickshire, on the 30th of January 1775— the anniversary of the execution of Charles I. He was educated at Rugby School and at Oxford; but his fierce and insubordinate temper— which remained with him, and injured him all his life— procured his expulsion from both of these places. As heir to a large estate, he resolved to give himself up entirely to literature; and he accordingly declined to adopt any profession. Living an almost purely intellectual life, he wrote a great deal of prose and some poetry; and his first volume of poems appeared before the close of the eighteenth century. His life, which began in the reign of George III., stretched through the reigns of George IV. and William IV., into the twenty-seventh year of Queen Victoria; and, in the course of this long life, he had manifold experiences, many loves and hates, friendships and acquaintanceships, with persons of every sort and rank. He joined the Spanish army to fight Napoleon, and presented the Spanish Government with large sums of money. He spent about thirty years of his life in Florence, where he wrote many of his works. He died at Florence in the year 1864. His greatest prose work is the Imaginary Conversations; his best poem is Count Julian; and the character of Count Julian has been ranked by De Quincey with the Satan of Milton. Some of his smaller poetic pieces are perfect; and there is one, Rose

Aylmer, written about a dear young friend, that Lamb was never tired of repeating:—

"Ah! what avails the sceptred race!
  Ah! what the form divine!
What every virtue, every grace!
  Rose Aylmer, all were thine!

"Rose Aylmer, whom these wakeful eyes
  Shall weep, but never see!
A night of memories and sighs
  I consecrate to thee."

25. JANE AUSTEN (1775-1817), the most delicate and faithful painter of English social life, was born at Steventon, in Hampshire, in 1775— in the same year as Landor and Lamb. She wrote a small number of novels, most of which are almost perfect in their minute and true painting of character. Sir Walter Scott, Macaulay, and other great writers, are among her fervent admirers. Scott says of her writing: "The big bow-wow strain I can do myself, like any now going; but the exquisite touch which renders ordinary commonplace things and characters interesting, from the truth of the description and the sentiment, is denied to me." She works out her characters by making them reveal themselves in their talk, and by an infinite series of minute touches. Her two best novels are Emma and Pride and Prejudice. The interest of them depends on the truth of the painting; and many thoughtful persons read through the whole of her novels every year.

26. THOMAS DE QUINCEY (1785-1859), one of our most brilliant essayists, was born at Greenhays, Manchester, in the year 1785. He was educated at the Manchester grammar-school and at Worcester College, Oxford. While at Oxford he took little share in the regular studies of his college, but read enormous numbers of Greek, Latin, and English books, as his taste or whim suggested. He knew no one; he hardly knew his own tutor. "For the first two years of my residence in Oxford," he says, "I compute that I did not utter one hundred words." After leaving Oxford, he lived for about twenty years in the Lake country; and there he became acquainted with Wordsworth, Hartley Coleridge (the son of S. T. Coleridge), and John Wilson (afterwards known as Professor Wilson, and also as the "Christopher North" of 'Blackwood's Magazine'). Suffering from repeated attacks of neuralgia, he gradually formed the habit of taking laudanum; and by the time he had reached the age of thirty, he drank about 8000 drops a-day. This unfortunate habit injured his powers of work and weakened his will. In spite of it, however, he wrote many hundreds of essays and articles in reviews and magazines. In the latter part of his life, he lived either near or in Edinburgh, and was always employed in dreaming (the opium increased his power both of dreaming and of musing), or in studying or writing. He died in Edinburgh in the year 1859. —Many of his essays were written under

the signature of "The English Opium-Eater." Probably his best works are The Confessions of an Opium-Eater and The Vision of Sudden Death. The chief characteristics of his style are majestic rhythm and elaborate eloquence. Some of his sentences are almost as long and as sustained as those of Jeremy Taylor; while, in many passages of reasoning that glows and brightens with strong passion and emotion, he is not inferior to Burke. He possessed an enormous vocabulary— in wealth of words and phrases he surpasses both Macaulay and Carlyle; and he makes a very large— perhaps even an excessive— use of Latin words. He is also very fond of using metaphors, personifications, and other figures of speech. It may be said without exaggeration that, next to Carlyle's, De Quincey's style is the most stimulating and inspiriting that a young reader can find among modern writers.

27. THOMAS CARLYLE (1795-1881), a great thinker, essayist, and historian, was born at Ecclefechan, in Dumfriesshire, in the year 1795. He was educated at the burgh school of Annan, and afterwards at the University of Edinburgh. Classics and the higher mathematics were his favourite studies; and he was more especially fond of astronomy. He was a teacher for some years after leaving the University. For a few years after this he was engaged in minor literary work; and translating from the German occupied a good deal of his time. In 1826 he married Jane Welsh, a woman of abilities only inferior to his own. His first original work was Sartor Resartus ("The Tailor Repatched"), which appeared in 1834, and excited a great deal of attention— a book which has proved to many the electric spark which first woke into life their powers of thought and reflection. From 1837 to 1840 he gave courses of lectures in London; and these lectures were listened to by the best and most thoughtful of the London people. The most striking series afterwards appeared in the form of a book, under the title of Heroes and Hero-Worship. Perhaps his most remarkable book— a book that is unique in all English literature— is The French Revolution, which appeared in 1837. In the year 1845, his Cromwell's Letters and Speeches were published, and drew after them a large number of eager readers. In 1865 he completed the hardest piece of work he had ever undertaken, his History of Frederick II., commonly called the Great. This work is so highly regarded in Germany as a truthful and painstaking history that officers in the Prussian army are obliged to study it, as containing the best account of the great battles of the Continent, the fields on which they were fought, and the strategy that went to win them. One of the crowning external honours of Carlyle's life was his appointment as Lord Rector of the University of Edinburgh in 1866; but at the very time that he was delivering his famous and remarkable Installation Address, his wife lay dying in London. This stroke brought terrible sorrow on the old man; he never ceased to mourn for his loss, and to recall the virtues and the beauties of character in his dead wife; "the light of his life," he said, "was quite gone out;" and he wrote very little after her death. He himself died in London on the 5th of February 1881.

28. Carlyle's Style.— Carlyle was an author by profession, a teacher of and prophet to his countrymen by his mission, and a student of history by the deep

interest he took in the life of man. He was always more or less severe in his judgments— he has been called "The Censor of the Age,"— because of the high ideal which he set up for his own conduct and the conduct of others. —He shows in his historic writings a splendour of imagery and a power of dramatic grouping second only to Shakespeare's. In command of words he is second to no modern English writer. His style has been highly praised and also energetically blamed. It is rugged, gnarled, disjointed, full of irregular force— shot across by sudden lurid lights of imagination— full of the most striking and indeed astonishing epithets, and inspired by a certain grim Titanic force. His sentences are often clumsily built. He himself said of them: "Perhaps not more than nine-tenths stand straight on their legs; the remainder are in quite angular attitudes; a few even sprawl out helplessly on all sides, quite broken-backed and dismembered." There is no modern writer who possesses so large a profusion of figurative language. His works are also full of the pithiest and most memorable sayings, such as the following:—

"Genius is an immense capacity for taking pains."

"Do the duty which lies nearest thee! Thy second duty will already have become clearer."

"History is a mighty drama, enacted upon the theatre of time, with suns for lamps, and eternity for a background."

"All true work is sacred. In all true work, were it but true hand-labour, there is something of divineness. Labour, wide as the earth, has its summit in heaven."

"Remember now and always that Life is no idle dream, but a solemn reality based upon Eternity, and encompassed by Eternity. Find out your task: stand to it: the night cometh when no man can work."

29. THOMAS BABINGTON MACAULAY (1800-1859), the most popular of modern historians,— an essayist, poet, statesman, and orator,— was born at Rothley Temple, in Leicestershire, in the year 1800. His father was one of the greatest advocates for the abolition of slavery; and received, after his death, the honour of a monument in Westminster Abbey. Young Macaulay was educated privately, and then at Trinity College, Cambridge. He studied classics with great diligence and success, but detested mathematics— a dislike the consequences of which he afterwards deeply regretted. In 1824 he was elected Fellow of his college. His first literary work was done for Knight's 'Quarterly Magazine'; but the earliest piece of writing that brought him into notice was his famous essay on Milton, written for the 'Edinburgh Review' in 1825. Several years of his life were spent in India, as Member of the Supreme Council; and, on his return, he entered Parliament, where he sat as M.P. for Edinburgh. Several offices were filled by him, among others that of Paymaster-General of the Forces, with a seat in the Cabinet of Lord John Russell. In 1842 appeared his Lays of Ancient

Rome, poems which have found a very large number of readers. His greatest work is his History of England from the Accession of James II. To enable himself to write this history he read hundreds of books, Acts of Parliament, thousands of pamphlets, tracts, broadsheets, ballads, and other flying fragments of literature; and he never seems to have forgotten anything he ever read. In. 1849 he was elected Lord Rector of the University of Glasgow; and in 1857 was raised to the peerage with the title of Baron Macaulay of Rothley— the first literary man who was ever called to the House of Lords. He died at Holly Lodge, Kensington, in the year 1859.

30. Macaulay's Style.— One of the most remarkable qualities in his style is the copiousness of expression, and the remarkable power of putting the same statement in a large number of different ways. This enormous command of expression corresponded with the extraordinary power of his memory. At the age of eight he could repeat the whole of Scott's poem of "Marmion." He was fond, at this early age, of big words and learned English; and once, when he was asked by a lady if his toothache was better, he replied, "Madam, the agony is abated!" He knew the whole of Homer and of Milton by heart; and it was said with perfect truth that, if Milton's poetical works could have been lost, Macaulay would have restored every line with complete exactness. Sydney Smith said of him: "There are no limits to his knowledge, on small subjects as on great; he is like a book in breeches." His style has been called "abrupt, pointed, and oratorical." He is fond of the arts of surprise— of antithesis— and of epigram. Sentences like these are of frequent occurrence:—

"Cranmer could vindicate himself from the charge of being a heretic only by arguments which made him out to be a murderer."

"The Puritan hated bear-baiting, not because it gave pain to the bear, but because it gave pleasure to the spectators."

Besides these elements of epigram and antithesis, there is a vast wealth of illustration, brought from the stores of a memory which never seemed to forget anything. He studied every sentence with the greatest care and minuteness, and would often rewrite paragraphs and even whole chapters, until he was satisfied with the variety and clearness of the expression. "He could not rest," it was said, "until the punctuation was correct to a comma; until every paragraph concluded with a telling sentence, and every sentence flowed like clear running water." But, above all things, he strove to make his style perfectly lucid and immediately intelligible. He is fond of countless details; but he so masters and marshals these details that each only serves to throw more light upon the main statement. His prose may be described as pictorial prose. The character of his mind was, like Burke's, combative and oratorical; and he writes with the greatest vigour and animation when he is attacking a policy or an opinion.

CHAPTER IX.

THE SECOND HALF OF THE NINETEENTH CENTURY.

1. Science.— The second half of the nineteenth century is distinguished by the enormous advance made in science, and in the application of science to the industries and occupations of the people. Chemistry and electricity have more especially made enormous strides. Within the last twenty years, chemistry has remade itself into a new science; and electricity has taken a very large part of the labour of mankind upon itself. It carries our messages round the world— under the deepest seas, over the highest mountains, to every continent, and to every great city; it lights up our streets and public halls; it drives our engines and propels our trains. But the powers of imagination, the great literary powers of poetry, and of eloquent prose,— especially in the domain of fiction,— have not decreased because science has grown. They have rather shown stronger developments. We must, at the same time, remember that a great deal of the literary work published by the writers who lived, or are still living, in the latter half of this century, was written in the former half. Thus, Longfellow was a man of forty-three, and Tennyson was forty-one, in the year 1850; and both had by that time done a great deal of their best work. The same is true of the prose-writers, Thackeray, Dickens, and Ruskin.

2. Poets and Prose-Writers.— The six greatest poets of the latter half of this century are Longfellow, a distinguished American poet, Tennyson, Mrs Browning, Robert Browning, William Morris, and Matthew Arnold. Of these, Mrs Browning and Longfellow are dead— Mrs Browning having died in 1861, and Longfellow in 1882. —The four greatest writers of prose are Thackeray, Dickens, George Eliot, and Ruskin. Of these, only Ruskin is alive.

3. HENRY WADSWORTH LONGFELLOW (1807-1882), the most popular of American poets, and as popular in Great Britain as he is in the United States, was born at Portland, Maine, in the year 1807. He was educated at Bowdoin College, and took his degree there in the year 1825. His profession was to have been the law; but, from the first, the whole bent of his talents and character was literary. At the extraordinary age of eighteen the professorship of modern languages in his own college was offered to him; it was eagerly accepted, and in order to qualify himself for his duties, he spent the next four years in Germany, France, Spain, and Italy. His first important prose work was Outre-Mer, or a Pilgrimage beyond the Sea. In 1837 he was offered the Chair of Modern Languages and Literature in Harvard University, and he again paid a visit to Europe— this time giving his thoughts and study chiefly to Germany, Denmark, and Scandinavia. In 1839 he published the prose romance called Hyperion. But it was not as a prose-writer that Longfellow gained the secure place he has in the hearts of the English-speaking peoples; it was as a poet. His first volume of poems was called Voices of the Night, and appeared in 1841; Evangeline was published in 1848; and Hiawatha, on which his poetical reputation is perhaps most firmly based, in 1855. Many other volumes of

poetry— both original and translations— have also come from his pen; but these are the best. The University of Oxford created him Doctor of Civil Law in 1869. He died at Harvard in the year 1882. A man of singularly mild and gentle character, of sweet and charming manners, his own lines may be applied to him with perfect appropriateness—

"His gracious presence upon earth
Was as a fire upon a hearth;
As pleasant songs, at morning sung,
The words that dropped from his sweet tongue
Strengthened our hearts, or— heard at night—
Made all our slumbers soft and light."

4. Longfellow's Style.— In one of his prose works, Longfellow himself says, "In character, in manners, in style, in all things, the supreme excellence is simplicity." This simplicity he steadily aimed at, and in almost all his writings reached; and the result is the sweet lucidity which is manifest in his best poems. His verse has been characterised as "simple, musical, sincere, sympathetic, clear as crystal, and pure as snow." He has written in a great variety of measures— in more, perhaps, than have been employed by Tennyson himself. His "Evangeline" is written in a kind of dactylic hexameter, which does not always scan, but which is almost always musical and impressive—

"Fair was she and young, when in hope began the long journey; Faded was she and old, when in disappointment it ended."

The "Hiawatha," again, is written in a trochaic measure— each verse containing four trochees—

"'Farewell!' said he, 'Minnehaha,
Farewell, O my laughing water!
All my heart is buried with you,
All´ my thou´ghts go on´ward wi´th you!'"

He is always careful and painstaking with his rhythm and with the cadence of his verse. It may be said with truth that Longfellow has taught more people to love poetry than any other English writer, however great.

5. ALFRED TENNYSON, a great English poet, who has written beautiful poetry for more than fifty years, was born at Somersby, in Lincolnshire, in the year 1809. He is the youngest of three brothers, all of whom are poets. He was educated at Cambridge, and some of his poems have shown, in a striking light, the forgotten beauty of the fens and flats of Cambridge and Lincolnshire. In 1829 he obtained the Chancellor's medal for a poem on "Timbuctoo." In 1830 he published his first volume, with the title of Poems chiefly Lyrical— a volume which contained, among other beautiful verses, the "Recollections of the Arabian Nights" and "The Dying Swan." In 1833 he issued another volume, called simply Poems; and this contained the exquisite poems entitled "The

Miller's Daughter" and "The Lotos-Eaters." The Princess, a poem as remarkable for its striking thoughts as for its perfection of language, appeared in 1847. The In Memoriam, a long series of short poems in memory of his dear friend, Arthur Henry Hallam, the son of Hallam the historian, was published in the year 1850. When Wordsworth died in 1850, Tennyson was appointed to the office of Poet-Laureate. This office, from the time when Dryden was forced to resign it in 1689, to the time when Southey accepted it in 1813, had always been held by third or fourth rate writers; in the present day it is held by the man who has done the largest amount of the best poetical work. The Idylls of the King appeared in 1859. This series of poems— perhaps his greatest— contains the stories of "Arthur and the Knights of the Round Table." Many other volumes of poems have been given by him to the world. In his old age he has taken to the writing of ballads and dramas. His ballad of The Revenge is one of the noblest and most vigorous poems that England has ever seen. The dramas of Harold, Queen Mary, and Becket, are perhaps his best; and the last was written when the poet had reached the age of seventy-four. In the year 1882 he was created Baron Tennyson, and called to the House of Peers.

6. Tennyson's Style.— Tennyson has been to the last two generations of Englishmen the national teacher of poetry. He has tried many new measures; he has ventured on many new rhythms; and he has succeeded in them all. He is at home equally in the slowest, most tranquil, and most meditative of rhythms, and in the rapidest and most impulsive. Let us look at the following lines as an example of the first. The poem is written on a woman who is dying of a lingering disease—

"Fair is her cottage in its place,
  Where yon broad water sweetly slowly glides:
It sees itself from thatch to base
  Dream in the sliding tides.

"And fairer she: but, ah! how soon to die!
  Her quiet dream of life this hour may cease:
Her peaceful being slowly passes by
  To some more perfect peace."

The very next poem, "The Sailor Boy," in the same volume, is— though written in exactly the same measure— driven on with the most rapid march and vigorous rhythm—

"He rose at dawn and, fired with hope,
  Shot o'er the seething harbour-bar,
And reached the ship and caught the rope
  And whistled to the morning-star."

And this is a striking and prominent characteristic of all Tennyson's poetry. Everywhere the sound is made to be "an echo to the sense"; the style is in perfect keeping with the matter. In the "Lotos-Eaters," we have the sense of complete indolence and deep repose in—
"A land of streams! Some, like a downward smoke,
Slow-dropping veils of thinnest lawn, did go."
In the "Boädicea," we have the rush and the shock of battle, the closing of legions, the hurtle of arms and the clash of armed men—
"Phantom sound of blows descending, moan of an enemy massacred,
Phantom wail of women and children, multitudinous agonies."
Many of Tennyson's sweetest and most pathetic lines have gone right into the heart of the nation, such as—
"But oh for the touch of a vanished hand,
And the sound of a voice that is still!"
All his language is highly polished, ornate, rich— sometimes Spenserian in luxuriant imagery and sweet music, sometimes even Homeric in massiveness and severe simplicity. Thus, in the "Morte d'Arthur," he speaks of the knight walking to the lake as—
"Clothed with his breath, and looking as he walked, Larger than human on the frozen hills."
Many of his pithy lines have taken root in the memory of the English people, such as these—

"Tis better to have loved and lost,
Than never to have loved at all."
"For words, like Nature, half reveal,
And half conceal, the soul within."
"Kind hearts are more than coronets,
And simple faith than Norman blood."

7. ELIZABETH BARRETT BARRETT, afterwards MRS BROWNING, the greatest poetess of this century, was born in London in the year 1809. She wrote verses "at the age of eight— and earlier," she says; and her first volume of poems was published when she was seventeen. When still a girl, she broke a blood-vessel upon the lungs, was ordered to a warmer climate than that of London; and her brother, whom she loved very dearly, took her down to Torquay. There a terrible tragedy was enacted before her eyes. One day the weather and the water looked very tempting; her brother took a sailing-boat for a short cruise in Torbay; the boat went down in front of the house, and in view of his sister; the body was never recovered. This sad event completely destroyed her already weak health; she returned to London, and spent several years in a darkened room. Here she "read almost every book worth reading in almost every language, and gave herself heart and soul to that poetry of which she seemed born to be the priestess." This way of life lasted for many years: and, in the course of it, she published several volumes of noble verse. In 1846 she

married Robert Browning, also a great poet. In 1856 she brought out Aurora Leigh, her longest, and probably also her greatest, poem. Mr Ruskin called it "the greatest poem which the century has produced in any language;" but this is going too far. —Mrs Browning will probably be longest remembered by her incomparable sonnets and by her lyrics, which are full of pathos and passion. Perhaps her two finest poems in this kind are the Cry of the Children and Cowper's Grave. All her poems show an enormous power of eloquent, penetrating, and picturesque language; and many of them are melodious with a rich and wonderful music. She died in 1861.

8. ROBERT BROWNING, the most daring and original poet of the century, was born in Camberwell, a southern suburb of London, in the year 1812. He was privately educated. In 1836 he published his first poem Paracelsus, which many wondered at, but few read. It was the story of a man who had lost his way in the mazes of thought about life,— about its why and wherefore,— about this world and the next,— about himself and his relations to God and his fellow-men. Mr Browning has written many plays, but they are more fit for reading in the study than for acting on the stage. His greatest work is The Ring and the Book; and it is most probably by this that his name will live in future ages. Of his minor poems, the best known and most popular is The Pied Piper of Hamelin— a poem which is a great favourite with all young people, from the picturesqueness and vigour of the verse. The most deeply pathetic of his minor poems is Evelyn Hope:—

"So, hush,— I will give you this leaf to keep—
See, I shut it inside the sweet cold hand,
There! that is our secret! go to sleep;
You will wake, and remember, and understand."

9. Browning's Style.— Browning's language is almost always very hard to understand; but the meaning, when we have got at it, is well worth all the trouble that may have been taken to reach it. His poems are more full of thought and more rich in experience than those of any other English writer except Shakspeare. The thoughts and emotions which throng his mind at the same moment so crowd upon and jostle each other, become so inextricably intermingled, that it is very often extremely difficult for us to make out any meaning at all. Then many of his thoughts are so subtle and so profound that they cannot easily be drawn up from the depths in which they lie. No man can write with greater directness, greater lyric vigour, fire, and impulse, than Browning when he chooses— write more clearly and forcibly about such subjects as love and war; but it is very seldom that he does choose. The infinite complexity of human life and its manifold experiences have seized and imprisoned his imagination; and it is not often that he speaks in a clear, free voice.

10. MATTHEW ARNOLD, one of the finest poets and noblest stylists of the age, was born at Laleham, near Staines, on the Thames, in the year 1822. He is the eldest son of the great Dr Arnold, the famous Head-master of Rugby. He was educated at Winchester and Rugby, from which latter school he proceeded to Balliol College, Oxford. The Newdigate prize for English verse was won by him in 1843— the subject of his poem being Cromwell. His first volume of poems was published in 1848. In the year 1851 he was appointed one of H.M. Inspectors of Schools; and he held that office up to the year 1885. In 1857 he was elected Professor of Poetry in the University of Oxford. In 1868 appeared a new volume with the simple title of New Poems; and, since then, he has produced a large number of books, mostly in prose. He is no less famous as a critic than as a poet; and his prose is singularly beautiful and musical.

11. Arnold's Style.— The chief qualities of his verse are clearness, simplicity, strong directness, noble and musical rhythm, and a certain intense calm. His lines on Morality give a good idea of his style:—

"We cannot kindle when we will
The fire that in the heart resides:
The spirit bloweth and is still
In mystery our soul abides:
  But tasks in hours of insight willed
  Can be through hours of gloom fulfilled.

With aching hands and bleeding feet
We dig and heap, lay stone on stone;
We bear the burden and the heat
Of the long day, and wish 'twere done.
  Not till the hours of light return,
  All we have built do we discern."

His finest poem in blank verse is his Sohrab and Rustum— a tale of the Tartar wastes. One of his noblest poems, called Rugby Chapel, describes the strong and elevated character of his father, the Head-master of Rugby. —His prose is remarkable for its lucidity, its pleasant and almost conversational rhythm, and its perfection of language.

12. WILLIAM MORRIS, a great narrative poet, was born near London in the year 1834. He was educated at Marlborough and at Exeter College, Oxford. In 1858 appeared his first volume of poems. In 1863 he began a business for the production of artistic wall-paper, stained glass, and furniture; he has a shop for the sale of these works of art in Oxford Street, London; and he devotes most of his time to drawing and designing for artistic manufacturers. His first poem, The Life and Death of Jason, appeared in 1867; and his magnificent series of narrative poems— The Earthly Paradise— was published in the years from 1868 and 1870. 'The Earthly Paradise' consists of twenty-four tales in verse, set in a framework much like that of Chaucer's 'Canterbury Tales.' The poetic power in

these tales is second only to that of Chaucer; and Morris has always acknowledged himself to be a pupil of Chaucer's—

"Thou, my Master still,
Whatever feet have climbed Parnassus' hill."

Mr Morris has also translated the Æneid of Virgil, and several works from the Icelandic.

13. Morris's Style.— Clearness, strength, music, picturesqueness, and easy flow, are the chief characteristics of Morris's style. Of the month of April he says:—

"O fair midspring, besung so oft and oft,
How can I praise thy loveliness enow?
Thy sun that burns not, and thy breezes soft
That o'er the blossoms of the orchard blow,
The thousand things that 'neath the young leaves grow
The hopes and chances of the growing year,
Winter forgotten long, and summer near."

His pictorial power— the power of bringing a person or a scene fully and adequately before one's eyes by the aid of words alone— is as great as that of Chaucer. The following is his picture of Edward III. in middle age:—

"Broad-browed he was, hook-nosed, with wide grey eyes
No longer eager for the coming prize,
But keen and steadfast: many an ageing line,
Half-hidden by his sweeping beard and fine,
Ploughed his thin cheeks; his hair was more than grey,
And like to one he seemed whose better day
Is over to himself, though foolish fame
Shouts louder year by year his empty name.
Unarmed he was, nor clad upon that morn
Much like a king: an ivory hunting-horn
Was slung about him, rich with gems and gold,
And a great white ger-falcon did he hold
Upon his fist; before his feet there sat
A scrivener making notes of this and that
As the King bade him, and behind his chair
His captains stood in armour rich and fair."

Morris's stores of language are as rich as Spenser's; and he has much the same copious and musical flow of poetic words and phrases.

14. WILLIAM MAKEPEACE THACKERAY (1811-1863), one of the most original of English novelists, was born at Calcutta in the year 1811. The son of a gentleman high in the civil service of the East India Company, he was sent to England to be educated, and was some years at Charterhouse School,

where one of his schoolfellows was Alfred Tennyson. He then went on to the University of Cambridge, which he left without taking a degree. Painting was the profession that he at first chose; and he studied art both in France and Germany. At the age of twenty-nine, however, he discovered that he was on a false tack, gave up painting, and took to literary work as his true field. He contributed many pleasant articles to 'Fraser's Magazine,' under the name of Michael Angelo Titmarsh; and one of his most beautiful and most pathetic stories, The Great Hoggarty Diamond, was also written under this name. He did not, however, take his true place as an English novelist of the first rank until the year 1847, when he published his first serial novel, Vanity Fair. Readers now began everywhere to class him with Charles Dickens, and even above him. His most beautiful work is perhaps The Newcomes; but the work which exhibits most fully the wonderful power of his art and his intimate knowledge of the spirit and the details of our older English life is The History of Henry Esmond— a work written in the style and language of the days of Queen Anne, and as beautiful as anything ever done by Addison himself. He died in the year 1863.

15. CHARLES DICKENS (1812-1870), the most popular writer of this century, was born at Landport, Portsmouth, in the year 1812. His delicate constitution debarred him from mixing in boyish sports, and very early made him a great reader. There was a little garret in his father's house where a small collection of books was kept; and, hidden away in this room, young Charles devoured such books as the 'Vicar of Wakefield,' 'Robinson Crusoe,' and many other famous English books. This was in Chatham. The family next removed to London, where the father was thrown into prison for debt. The little boy, weakly and sensitive, was now sent to work in a blacking manufactory at six shillings a-week, his duty being to cover the blacking-pots with paper. "No words can express," he says, "the secret agony of my soul, as I compared these my everyday associates with those of my happier childhood, and felt my early hopes of growing up to be a learned and distinguished man crushed in my breast.... The misery it was to my young heart to believe that, day by day, what I had learned, and thought, and delighted in, and raised my fancy and my emulation up by, was passing away from me, never to be brought back any more, cannot be written." When his father's affairs took a turn for the better, he was sent to school; but it was to a school where "the boys trained white mice much better than the master trained the boys." In fact, his true education consisted in his eager perusal of a large number of miscellaneous books. When he came to think of what he should do in the world, the profession of reporter took his fancy; and, by the time he was nineteen, he had made himself the quickest and most accurate— that is, the best reporter in the Gallery of the House of Commons. His first work, Sketches by Boz, was published in 1836. In 1837 appeared the Pickwick Papers; and this work at once lifted Dickens into the foremost rank as a popular writer of fiction. From this time he was almost constantly engaged in writing novels. His Oliver Twist and David Copperfield contain reminiscences of his own life; and perhaps the latter is his most powerful work. "Like many fond parents," he wrote, "I

have in my heart of hearts a favourite child; and his name is David Copperfield." He lived with all the strength of his heart and soul in the creations of his imagination and fancy while he was writing about them; he says himself, "No one can ever believe this narrative, in the reading, more than I believed it in the writing;" and each novel, as he wrote it, made him older and leaner. Great knowledge of the lives of the poor, and great sympathy with them, were among his most striking gifts; and Sir Arthur Helps goes so far as to say, "I doubt much whether there has ever been a writer of fiction who took such a real and living interest in the world about him." He died in the year 1870, and was buried in Westminster Abbey.

16. Dickens's Style.— His style is easy, flowing, vigorous, picturesque, and humorous; his power of language is very great; and, when he is writing under the influence of strong passion, it rises into a pure and noble eloquence. The scenery— the external circumstances of his characters, are steeped in the same colours as the characters themselves; everything he touches seems to be filled with life and to speak— to look happy or sorrowful,— to reflect the feelings of the persons. His comic and humorous powers are very great; but his tragic power is also enormous— his power of depicting the fiercest passions that tear the human breast,— avarice, hate, fear, revenge, remorse. The great American statesman, Daniel Webster, said that Dickens had done more to better the condition of the English poor than all the statesmen Great Britain had ever sent into the English Parliament.

17. JOHN RUSKIN, the greatest living master of English prose, an art-critic and thinker, was born in London in the year 1819. In his father's house he was accustomed "to no other prospect than that of the brick walls over the way; he had no brothers, nor sisters, nor companions." To his London birth he ascribes the great charm that the beauties of nature had for him from his boyhood: he felt the contrast between town and country, and saw what no country-bred child could have seen in sights that were usual to him from his infancy. He was educated at Christ Church, Oxford, and gained the Newdigate prize for poetry in 1839. He at first devoted himself to painting; but his true and strongest genius lay in the direction of literature. In 1843 appeared the first volume of his Modern Painters, which is perhaps his greatest work; and the four other volumes were published between that date and the year 1860. In this work he discusses the qualities and the merits of the greatest painters of the English, the Italian, and other schools. In 1851 he produced a charming fairy tale, 'The King of the Golden River, or the Black Brothers.' He has written on architecture also, on political economy, and on many other social subjects. He is the founder of a society called "The St George's Guild," the purpose of which is to spread abroad sound notions of what true life and true art are, and especially to make the life of the poor more endurable and better worth living.

18. Ruskin's Style.— A glowing eloquence, a splendid and full-flowing music, wealth of phrase, aptness of epithet, opulence of ideas— all these qualities characterise the prose style of Mr Ruskin. His similes are daring, but always true. Speaking of the countless statues that fill the innumerable niches of

the cathedral of Milan, he says that "it is as though a flight of angels had alighted there and been struck to marble." His writings are full of the wisest sayings put into the most musical and beautiful language. Here are a few:—

"Every act, every impulse, of virtue and vice, affects in any
creature, face, voice, nervous power, and vigour and harmony of
invention, at once. Perseverance in rightness of human conduct
renders, after a certain number of generations, human art possible;
every sin clouds it, be it ever so little a one; and persistent
vicious living and following of pleasure render, after a certain
number of generations, all art impossible."

"In mortals, there is a care for trifles, which proceeds from love
and conscience, and is most holy; and a care for trifles, which
comes of idleness and frivolity, and is most base. And so, also,
there is a gravity proceeding from dulness and mere incapability of
enjoyment, which is most base."

His power of painting in words is incomparably greater than that of any other English author: he almost infuses colour into his words and phrases, so full are they of pictorial power. It would be impossible to give any adequate idea of this power here; but a few lines may suffice for the present:—

"The noonday sun came slanting down the rocky slopes of La Riccia,
and its masses of enlarged and tall foliage, whose autumnal tints
were mixed with the wet verdure of a thousand evergreens, were
penetrated with it as with rain. I cannot call it colour; it was
conflagration. Purple, and crimson, and scarlet, like the curtains
of God's tabernacle, the rejoicing trees sank into the valley in
showers of light, every separate leaf quivered with buoyant and
burning life; each, as it turned to reflect or to transmit the
sunbeam, first a torch and then an emerald."

19. GEORGE ELIOT (the literary name for Marian Evans, 1819-1880), one of our greatest writers, was born in Warwickshire in the year 1819. She was well and carefully educated; and her own serious and studious character made her a careful thinker and a most diligent reader. For some time the famous Herbert Spencer was her tutor; and under his care her mind developed with surprising rapidity. She taught herself German, French, Italian— studied the best works in the literature of these languages; and she was also fairly mistress of Greek and Latin. Besides all these, she was an accomplished musician. —She was for some time assistant-editor of the 'Westminster Review.' The first of her works which called the attention of the public to her astonishing skill and power as a novelist was her Scenes of Clerical Life. Her most popular novel, Adam Bede, appeared in 1859; Romola in 1863; and Middlemarch in 1872. She has also written a good

deal of poetry, among other volumes that entitled The Legend of Jubal, and other Poems. One of her best poems is The Spanish Gypsy. She died in the year 1880.

20. George Eliot's Style.— Her style is everywhere pure and strong, of the best and most vigorous English, not only broad in its power, but often intense in its description of character and situation, and always singularly adequate to the thought. Probably no novelist knew the English character— especially in the Midlands— so well as she, or could analyse it with so much subtlety and truth. She is entirely mistress of the country dialects. In humour, pathos, knowledge of character, power of putting a portrait firmly upon the canvas, no writer surpasses her, and few come near her. Her power is sometimes almost Shakespearian. Like Shakespeare, she gives us a large number of wise sayings, expressed in the pithiest language. The following are a few:—

"It is never too late to be what you might have been."

"It is easy finding reasons why other people should be patient."

"Genius, at first, is little more than a great capacity for receiving discipline."

"Things are not so ill with you and me as they might have been, half
owing to the number who lived faithfully a hidden life, and rest in
unvisited tombs."

"Nature never makes men who are at once energetically sympathetic and minutely calculating."

"To the far woods he wandered, listening,
And heard the birds their little stories sing
In notes whose rise and fall seem melted speech—
Melted with tears, smiles, glances— that can reach
More quickly through our frame's deep-winding night,
And without thought raise thought's best fruit, delight."

TABLES OF ENGLISH LITERATURE.

[Note: In the original book, the following table— spanning 14 pages— was laid out in four columns: Writers; Works; Contemporary Events; Centuries (through 1500) or Decades (beginning 1550). Missing punctuation has been silently supplied.]

Centuries/Decades
 WRITERS
  Works
   Contemporary Events

   500
(Author unknown.)
Beowulf (brought over by Saxons and Angles from the Continent).
   600

 CAEDMON. A secular monk of Whitby. Died about 680.
  Poems on the Creation and other subjects taken from the Old and
  the New Testament.

   Edwin (of Deira), King of the Angles, baptised 627.

   700

 BAEDA. 672-735. "The Venerable Bede," a monk of Jarrow-on-Tyne.
  An Ecclesiastical History in Latin. A translation of St John's
  Gospel into English (lost).

   First landing of the Danes, 787.

   800

 ALFRED THE GREAT. 849-901. King; translator; prose-writer.
  Translated into the English of Wessex, Bede's Ecclesiastical History
  and other Latin works. Is said to have begun the Anglo-Saxon
  Chronicle.

   The University of Oxford is said to have been founded in this reign.
Compiled by monks in various monasteries.
Anglo-Saxon Chronicle, 875-1154.
   900
ASSER. Bishop of Sherborne. Died 910.
Life of King Alfred.
   1000

(Author unknown.)
A poem entitled The Grave.
   1100

  LAYAMON. 1150-1210. A priest of Ernley-on-Severn.
   The Brut (1205), a poem on Brutus, the supposed first settler in
   Britain.

   John ascended the throne in 1199.
     ORM or ORMIN. 1187-1237. A canon of the Order of St Augustine. The
Ormulum (1215), a set of religious services in metre.

   1200
ROBERT OF GLOUCESTER. 1255-1307.
Chronicle of England in rhyme (1297).
Magna Charta, 1215.
Henry III. ascends the throne, 1216.
     ROBERT OF BRUNNE. (Robert Manning of Brun.) 1272-1340. Chronicle
of England in rhyme; Handlyng Sinne (1303).

   University of Cambridge founded, 1231.
   Edward I. ascends the throne, 1272.
   Conquest of Wales, 1284.

   1300

  SIR JOHN MANDEVILLE. 1300-1372. Physician; traveller; prose-writer.
   The Voyaige and Travaile. Travels to Jerusalem, India, and other
   countries, written in Latin French and English (1356). The first
   writer "in formed English."

Edward II ascends the throne, 1307.
Battle of Bannockburn, 1314.
  JOHN BARBOUR. Archdeacon of Aberdeen. 1316-1396.
   The Bruce (1377), a poem written in the Northern English or
   "Scottish" dialect.

   Edward III. ascends the throne, 1327.

1350

JOHN WYCLIF. 1324-1384. Vicar of Lutterworth, in Leicestershire.
Translation of the Bible from the Latin version; and many tracts
and pamphlets on Church reform.

Hundred Years' War begins, 1338.
Battle of Crecy, 1346.
JOHN GOWER. 1325-1408. A country gentleman of Kent; probably also a
lawyer.
Vox Clamantis, Confessio Amantis, Speculum Meditantis (1393);
and poems in French and Latin.

The Black Death, 1349, 1361, 1369.
WILLIAM LANGLANDE. 1332-1400. Born in Shropshire. Vision
concerning Piers the Plowman— three editions (1362-78).
Battle of Poitiers, 1356.
First law-pleadings in English, 1362.

GEOFFREY CHAUCER 1340-1400. Poet; courtier; soldier; diplomatist;
Comptroller of the Customs: Clerk of the King's Works; M.P.
The Canterbury Tales (1384-98), of which the best is the Knightes
Tale. Dryden called him "a perpetual fountain of good sense."

Richard II. ascends the throne, 1377.
Wat Tyler's insurrection, 1381.
JAMES I. OF SCOTLAND. 1394-1437. Prisoner in England, and educated
there, in 1405.
The King's Quair (= Book), a poem in the style of Chaucer.

Henry IV. ascends the throne, 1399.
1400

WILLIAM CAXTON. 1422-1492. Mercer; printer; translator;
prose-writer.
The Game and Playe of the Chesse (1474)— the first book printed
in England; Lives of the Fathers, "finished on the last day of his
life;" and many other works.

Henry V. ascends the throne, 1415.
Battle of Agincourt, 1415.
Henry VI. ascends the throne, 1422.
Invention of Printing, 1438-45.

1450

WILLIAM DUNBAR. 1450-1530. Franciscan or Grey Friar; Secretary to a
Scotch embassy to France.

The Golden Terge (1501); the Dance of the Seven Deadly Sins
(1507); and other poems. He has been called "the Chaucer of
Scotland."

Jack Cade's insurrection, 1450.
End of the Hundred Years' War, 1453.

GAWAIN DOUGLAS. 1474-1522. Bishop of Dunkeld, in Perthshire.
Palace of Honour (1501); translation of Virgil's Æneid (1513)—
the first translation of any Latin author into verse. Douglas wrote
in Northern English.

Wars of the Roses, 1455-86.
Edward IV. ascends the throne, 1461.

WILLIAM TYNDALE. 1477-1536. Student of theology; translator. Burnt
at Antwerp for heresy.

New Testament translated (1525-34); the Five Books of Moses
translated (1530). This translation is the basis of the Authorised
Version.

Edward V. king, 1483.

SIR THOMAS MORE. 1480-1535. Lord High Chancellor; writer on social
topics; historian.

History of King Edward V., and of his brother, and of Richard
III. (1513); Utopia (= "The Land of Nowhere"), written in Latin;
and other prose works.

Richard III. ascends the throne, 1483.
Battle of Bosworth, 1485.

SIR DAVID LYNDESAY. 1490-1556. Tutor of Prince James of Scotland
(James V.); "Lord Lyon King-at-Arms;" poet.

Lyndesay's Dream (1528); The Complaint (1529); A Satire of the
Three Estates (1535)— a "morality-play."

Henry VII. ascends the throne, 1485.
Greek began to be taught in England about 1497.

1500

ROGER ASCHAM. 1515-1568. Lecturer on Greek at Cambridge; tutor to
Edward VI., Queen Elizabeth, and Lady Jane Grey.
  Toxophilus (1544), a treatise on shooting with the bow; The
  Scholemastre (1570). "Ascham is plain and strong in his style, but
  without grace or warmth."

  Henry VIII. ascends the throne, 1509.
  Battle of Flodden, 1513.
  Wolsey Cardinal and Lord High Chancellor, 1515.

JOHN FOXE. 1517-1587. An English clergyman. Corrector for the press
at Basle; Prebendary of Salisbury Cathedral; prose-writer.
  The Book of Martyrs (1563), an account of the chief Protestant
  martyrs.

  Sir Thomas More first layman who was Lord High Chancellor, 1529.
Reformation in England begins about 1534.

EDMUND SPENSER. 1552-1599. Secretary to Viceroy of Ireland;
political writer; poet.
  Shepheard's Calendar (1579): Faerie Queene, in six books
  (1590-96).

Edward VI. ascends the throne, 1547.
Mary Tudor ascends the throne, 1553.

  1550

SIR WALTER RALEIGH. 1552-1618. Courtier; statesman; sailor;
coloniser; historian.
  History of the World (1614), written during the author's
  imprisonment in the Tower of London.

  Cranmer burnt 1556.

RICHARD HOOKER. 1553-1600. English clergyman; Master of the Temple;
Rector of Boscombe, in the diocese of Salisbury.
  Laws of Ecclesiastical Polity (1594). This book is an eloquent
  defence of the Church of England. The writer, from his excellent
  judgment, is generally called "the judicious Hooker."

  Elizabeth ascends the throne, 1558.

SIR PHILIP SIDNEY. 1554-1586. Courtier; general; romance-writer.
Arcadia, a romance (1580). Defence of Poesie, published after
his death (in 1595). Sonnets.

1560

FRANCIS BACON. 1561-1626. Viscount St Albans; Lord High Chancellor
of England; lawyer; philosopher; essayist.
Essays (1597); Advancement of Learning (1605); Novum Organum
(1620); and other works on methods of inquiry into nature.

Hawkins begins slave trade in 1562.
Rizzio murdered, 1566.
WILLIAM SHAKESPEARE. 1564-1616. Actor; owner of theatre;
play-writer; poet. Born and died at Stratford-on-Avon.
Thirty-seven plays. His greatest tragedies are Hamlet, Lear,
and Othello. His best comedies are Midsummer Night's Dream,
The Merchant of Venice, and As You Like It. His best historical
plays are Julius Cæsar and Richard III. Many minor poems—
chiefly sonnets. He wrote no prose.

Marlowe, Dekker, Chapman, Beaumont and Fletcher, Ford, Webster,
Ben Johnson, and other dramatists, were contemporaries of
Shakspeare.

1570

BEN JONSON. 1574-1637. Dramatist; poet; prose-writer.
Tragedies and comedies. Best plays: Volpone or the Fox; Every
Man in his Humour.

Drake sails round the world, 1577.
Execution of Mary Queen of Scots, 1578.

1580

WILLIAM DRUMMOND ("of Hawthornden"). 1585-1649. Scottish poet;
friend of Ben Jonson.
Sonnets and poems.

Raleigh in Virginia, 1584.
Babington's Plot, 1586.
Spanish Armada, 1588.

1590

THOMAS HOBBES. 1588-1679. Philosopher; prose-writer; translator of
Homer.
The Leviathan (1651), a work on politics and moral philosophy.

Battle of Ivry, 1590.
1600

SIR THOMAS BROWNE. 1605-1682. Physician at Norwich.
Religio Medici (= "The Religion of a Physician"); Urn-Burial;
and other prose works.

Australia discovered, 1601.
James I. ascends the throne in 1603.
JOHN MILTON. 1608-1674. Student; political writer; poet; Foreign (or
"Latin") Secretary to Cromwell. Became blind from over-work in 1654.
Minor Poems; Paradise Lost; Paradise Regained; Samson
Agonistes. Many prose works, the best being Areopagitica, a
speech for the Liberty of Unlicensed Printing.

Hampton Court Conference for translation of Bible, 1604-11. Gunpowder
Plot, 1605.
1610

SAMUEL BUTLER. 1612-1680. Literary man; secretary to the Earl of
Carbery.
Hudibras, a mock-heroic poem, written to ridicule the Puritan and
Parliamentarian party.

Execution of Raleigh, 1618.

JEREMY TAYLOR. 1613-1667. English clergyman; Bishop of Down and
Connor in Ireland.
Holy Living and Holy Dying (1649); and a number of other
religious books.

1620

JOHN BUNYAN. 1628-1688. Tinker and traveling preacher.
The Pilgrim's Progress (1678); the Holy War; and other religious
works.

Charles I. ascends the throne in 1625.
Petition of Right, 1628.

1630

JOHN DRYDEN. 1631-1700. Poet-Laureate and Historiographer-Royal; playwright; poet; prose-writer.
   Annus Mirabilis (= "The Wonderful Year," 1665-66, on the Plague and the Fire of London); Absalom and Achitophel (1681), a poem on political parties; Hind and Panther (1687), a religious poem. He also wrote many plays, some odes and a translation of Virgil's Æneid. His prose consists chiefly of prefaces and introductions to his poems.

No Parliament from 1629-40.
Scottish National Covenant, 1638.

1640

   Long Parliament, 1640-53.
   Marston Moor, 1644.
   Execution of Charles I., 1649.

1650

JOHN LOCKE. 1632-1704. Diplomatist; Secretary to the Board of Trade; philosopher; prose-writer.
   Essay concerning the Human Understanding (1690); Thoughts on Education; and other prose works.

The Commonwealth, 1649-60.
Cromwell Lord Protector, 1653-58.

1660

DANIEL DEFOE. 1661-1731. Literary man; pamphleteer; journalist; member of Commission on Union with Scotland.
   The True-born Englishman (1701); Robinson Crusoe (1719); Journal of the Plague (1722); and more than a hundred books in all.

   Restoration, 1660.
   First standing army, 1661.
   First newspaper in England, 1663.

JONATHAN SWIFT. 1667-1745. English clergyman; literary man; satirist; prose-writer; poet; Dean of St Patrick's, in Dublin.
   Battle of the Books; Tale of a Tub (1704), an allegory on the

Churches of Rome, England, and Scotland; Gulliver's Travels (1726); a few poems; and a number of very vigorous political pamphlets.

Plague of London, 1665.
Fire of London, 1666.

1670

SIR RICHARD STEELE. 1671-1729. Soldier; literary man; courtier; journalist; M.P.
Steele founded the 'Tatler,' 'Spectator,' 'Guardian,' and other small journals. He also wrote some plays.

Charles II. pensioned by Louis XIV. of France, 1674.

JOSEPH ADDISON. 1672-1719. Essayist; poet; Secretary of State for the Home Department.
Essays in the 'Tatler,' 'Spectator,' and 'Guardian.' Cato, a Tragedy (1713). Several Poems and Hymns.

The Habeas Corpus Act, 1679.

1680

ALEXANDER POPE. 1688-1744. Poet.
Essay on Criticism (1711); Rape of the Lock (1714); Translation of Homer's Iliad and Odyssey, finished in 1726; Dunciad (1729); Essay on Man (1739). A few prose Essays, and a volume of Letters.

James II. ascends the throne in 1685.
Revolution of 1688.
William III. and Mary II. ascend the throne, 1689.

1690
Battle of the Boyne, 1690.

JAMES THOMSON. 1700-1748. Poet.
The Seasons; a poem in blank verse (1730); The Castle of Indolence; a mock-heroic poem in the Spenserian stanza (1748).

Censorship of the Press abolished, 1695.
Queen Anne ascends the throne in 1702.

1700

HENRY FIELDING. 1707-1754. Police-magistrate, journalist; novelist.
  Joseph Andrews (1742); Amelia (1751). He was "the first great
  English novelist."

Battle of Blenheim, 1704.
Gibraltar taken, 1704.
DR SAMUEL JOHNSON. 1709-1784. Schoolmaster; literary man; essayist;
  poet; dictionary-maker.
    London (1738); The Vanity of Human Wishes (1749); Dictionary
    of the English Language (1755); Rasselas (1759); Lives of the
    Poets (1781). He also wrote The Idler, The Rambler, and a play
    called Irene.

  Union of England and Scotland, 1707.

  1710

DAVID HUME. 1711-1776. Librarian; Secretary to the French Embassy;
  philosopher; literary man.
    History of England (1754-1762); and a number of philosophical
    Essays. His prose is singularly clear, easy, and pleasant.

  George I. ascends the throne in 1714.

THOMAS GRAY. 1716-1771. Student; poet; letter-writer; Professor of
  Modern History in the University of Cambridge.
    Odes; Elegy Written in a Country Churchyard (1750)— one of the
    most perfect poems in our language. He was a great stylist, and an
    extremely careful workman.

  Rebellion in Scotland in 1715.

  1720

TOBIAS GEORGE SMOLLETT. 1721-1771. Doctor; pamphleteer; literary
  hack; novelist.
    Roderick Random (1748); Humphrey Clinker (1771). He also
    continued Hume's History of England. He published also some
    Plays and Poems.

  South-Sea Bubble bursts, 1720.

OLIVER GOLDSMITH. 1728-1774. Literary man; play-writer; poet.

The Traveller (1764); The Vicar of Wakefield (1766); The Deserted Village (1770); She Stoops to Conquer—a Play (1773); and a large number of books, pamphlets, and compilations.

George II. ascends the throne, 1727.

ADAM SMITH. 1723-1790. Professor in the University of Glasgow. Theory of Moral Sentiments (1759); Inquiry into the Nature and Causes of the Wealth of Nations (1776). He was the founder of the science of political economy.

1730

EDMUND BURKE. 1730-1797. M.P.; statesman; "the first man in the House of Commons;" orator; writer on political philosophy. Essay on the Sublime and Beautiful (1757); Reflections on the Revolution of France (1790); Letters on a Regicide Peace (1797); and many other works. "The greatest philosopher in practice the world ever saw."

WILLIAM COWPER. 1731-1800. Commissioner in Bankruptcy; Clerk of the Journals of the House of Lords; poet. Table Talk (1782); John Gilpin (1785); A Translation of Homer (1791); and many other Poems. His Letters, like Gray's, are among the best in the language.

1740

EDWARD GIBBON. 1737-1794. Historian; M.P. Decline and Fall of the Roman Empire (1776-87). "Heavily laden style and monotonous balance of every sentence."

Rebellion in Scotland, 1745, commonly called "The 'Forty-five." 1750

ROBERT BURNS. 1759-1796. Farm-labourer; ploughman; farmer; excise-officer; lyrical poet. Poems and Songs (1786-96). His prose consists chiefly of Letters. "His pictures of social life, of quaint humour, come up to nature; and they cannot go beyond it."

Clive in India, 1750-60.
Earthquake at Lisbon, 1755.
Black Hole of Calcutta, 1756.

1760

WILLIAM WORDSWORTH. 1770-1850. Distributor of Stamps for the county
  of Westmoreland; poet; poet-laureate.
    Lyrical Ballads (with Coleridge, 1798); The Excursion (1814);
    Yarrow Revisited (1835), and many poems. The Prelude was
    published after his death. His prose, which is very good, consists
    chiefly of Prefaces and Introductions.

George III. ascends the throne in 1760.
Napoleon and Wellington born, 1769.
  1770

SIR WALTER SCOTT. 1771-1832. Clerk to the Court of Session in
Edinburgh; Scottish barrister; poet; novelist.
    Lay of the Last Minstrel (1805); Marmion (1808); Lady of the
    Lake (1810); Waverley— the first of the "Waverley Novels"— was
    published in 1814. The "Homer of Scotland." His prose is bright and
    fluent, but very inaccurate.

  Warren Hastings in India, 1772-85.

SAMUEL TAYLOR COLERIDGE. 1772-1834. Private soldier; journalist;
literary man; philosopher; poet.
    The Ancient Mariner (1798); Christabel (1816); The Friend—
    a Collection of Essays (1812); Aids to Reflection (1825). His
    prose is very full both of thought and emotion.

ROBERT SOUTHEY. 1774-1843. Literary man; Quarterly Reviewer;
historian; poet-laureate.
    Joan of Arc (1796); Thalaba the Destroyer (1801); The Curse of
    Kehama (1810); A History of Brazil; The Doctor— a Collection
    of Essays; Life of Nelson. He wrote more than a hundred volumes.
    He was "the most ambitious and and most voluminous author of his
    age."

  American Declaration of Independence, 1776.

CHARLES LAMB. 1775-1834. Clerk in the East India House; poet;
prose-writer.
    Poems (1797); Tales from Shakespeare (1806); The Essays of
    Elia (1823-1833). One of the finest writers of writers of prose in
    the English language.

WALTER SAVAGE LANDOR. 1775-1864. Poet; prose-writer.
Gebir (1798); Count Julian (1812); Imaginary Conversations
(1824-1846); Dry Sticks Faggoted (1858). He wrote books for more
than sixty years. His style is full of vigour and sustained
eloquence.

Alliance of France and America, 1778.

THOMAS CAMPBELL. 1777-1844. Poet; literary man; editor.
The Pleasures of Hope (1799); Poems (1803); Gertrude of
Wyoming, Battle of the Baltic, Hohenlinden, etc. (1809). He
also wrote some Historical Works.

Encyclopædia Britannica founded in 1778.

HENRY HALLAM. 1778-1859. Historian.
View of Europe during the Middle Ages (1818); Constitutional
History of England (1827); Introduction to the Literature of
Europe (1839).

THOMAS MOORE. 1779-1852. Poet; prose-writer.
Odes and Epistles (1806); Lalla Rookh (1817); History of
Ireland (1827); Life of Byron (1830); Irish Melodies (1834);
and many prose works.

1780

THOMAS DE QUINCEY. 1785-1859. Essayist.
Confessions of an English Opium-Eater (1821). He wrote also on
many subjects— philosophy, poetry, classics, history, politics. His
writings fill twenty volumes. He was one of the finest prose-writers
of this century.

French Revolution begun in 1789.

LORD BYRON (George Gordon). 1788-1824. Peer; poet; volunteer to
Greece.
Hours of Idleness (1807); English Bards and Scotch Reviewers
(1809); Childe Harold's Pilgrimage (1812-1818); Hebrew Melodies
(1815); and many Plays. His prose, which is full of vigour and
animal spirits, is to be found chiefly in his Letters.

Bastille overthrown, 1789.
1790

PERCY BYSSHE SHELLEY. 1792-1822. Poet.
Queen Mab (1810); Prometheus Unbound—a Tragedy (1819); Ode to the Skylark, The Cloud (1820); Adonaïs (1821), and many other poems; and several prose works.

Cape of Good Hope Hope taken, 1795.
Bonaparte in Italy, 1796.
Battle of the Nile, 1798.

1800

JOHN KEATS. 1795-1821. Poet.
Poems (1817); Endymion (1818); Hyperion (1820). "Had Keats lived to the ordinary age of man, he would have been one of the greatest of all poets."

Union of Great Britain and Ireland, 1801.
Trafalgar and Nelson, 1805.

1810
Peninsular War, 1808-14.
Napoleon's Invasion of Russia; Moscow burnt, 1812.

1820

THOMAS CARLYLE. 1795-1881. Literary man; poet; translator; essayist; reviewer; political writer; historian.
German Romances— a set of Translations (1827); Sartor Resartus— "The Tailor Repatched" (1834); The French Revolution (1837); Heroes and Hero-Worship (1840); Past and Present (1843); Cromwell's Letters and Speeches (1845); Life of Frederick the Great (1858-65). "With the gift of song, Carlyle would have been the greatest of epic poets since Homer."

War with United States, 1812-14.
Battle of Waterloo,1815.

1830

George IV. ascends the throne, 1820.
Greek War of Freedom, 1822-29.
Byron in Greece, 1823-24.
Catholic Emancipation, 1829.

LORD MACAULAY (Thomas Babington). 1800-1859. Barrister; Edinburgh
Reviewer; M.P.; Member of the Supreme Council of India; Cabinet
Minister; poet; essayist; historian; peer.
  Milton (in the 'Edinburgh Review,' 1825); Lays of Ancient Rome
  (1842); History of England— unfinished (1849-59). "His pictorial
  faculty is amazing."

William IV. ascends the throne, 1830.
The Reform Bill, 1832.
Total Abolition of Slavery, 1834.

LORD LYTTON (Edward Bulwer). 1805-1873. Novelist; poet; dramatist;
M.P.; Cabinet Minister; peer.
  Ismael and Other Poems (1825); Eugene Aram (1831); Last Days of
  Pompeii (1834); The Caxtons (1849); My Novel (1853); Poems
  (1865).

Queen Victoria ascends the throne, 1837.

1840
Irish Famine, 1845.

JOHN STUART MILL. 1806-1873. Clerk in the East India House;
philospher; political writer; M.P.; Lord Rector of the University of
St Andrews.
  System of Logic (1843); Principles of Political Economy (1848);
  Essay on Liberty (1858); Autobiography (1873); "For judicial
  calmness, elevation of tone, and freedom from personality, Mill is
  unrivalled among the writers of his time."

Repeal of the Corn Laws, 1846.

1850
Revolution in Paris, 1851.
Death of Wellington, 1852.

HENRY W. LONGFELLOW. 1807-1882. Professor of Modern Languages and Literature in Harvard University, U.S.; poet; prose-writer.

Outre-Mer—a Story (1835); Hyperion—a Story (1839); Voices of the Night (1841); Evangeline (1848) Hiawatha (1855); Aftermath (1873). "His tact in the use of language is probably the chief cause of his success."

Napoleon III. Emperor of the French, 1852.
Russian War, 1854-56.

LORD TENNYSON (Alfred Tennyson). 1809———. Poet; poet-laureate; peer.

Poems (1830) In Memoriam (1850); Maud (1855); Idylls of the King (1859-73); Queen Mary—a Drama (1875); Becket—a Drama (1884). He is at present our greatest living poet.

Franco-Austrian War, 1859.

1860
Emancipation of Russian serfs, 1861.

ELIZABETH B. BARRETT (afterwards Mrs Browning). 1809-1861. Poet; prose-writer; translator.

Prometheus Bound— translated from the Greek of Æschylus (1833); Poems (1844); Aurora Leigh (1856); and Essays contributed to various magazines.

Austro-Prussian "Seven Weeks' War", 1866.
Suez canal finished, 1869.

1870

WILLIAM MAKEPEACE THACKERAY. 1811-1863. Novelist; writer in 'Punch';
artist.

The Paris Sketch-Book (1840); Vanity Fair (1847); Esmond (1852); The Newcomes(1855); The Virginians (1857). The greatest novelist and one of the most perfect stylists of this century. "The classical English humorist and satirist of the reign of Queen Victoria."

Franco-Prussian War 1870-71.
Third French Republic, 1870.
William I. of Prussia made Emperor of the Germans at Versailles, 1871.

CHARLES DICKENS. 1812-1870. Novelist.
Sketches by Boz (1836); The Pickwick Papers (1837); Oliver
Twist (1838); Nicholas Nickleby (1838); and many other novels and
works; Great Expectations (1868). The most popular writer that
ever lived.

Rome the new capital of Italy, 1871.
Russo-Turkish War 1877-78.
Berlin Congress and Treaty, 1878.

ROBERT BROWNING. 1812———. Poet.
Pauline (1833); Paracelsus (1836); Poems (1865); The Ring and
the Book (1869); and many other volumes of poetry.

Leo XIII. made Pope in 1878.

1880

JOHN RUSKIN. 1819———. Art-critic; essayist; teacher; literary man.
Modern Painters (1843-60); The Stones of Venice (1851-53); The
Queen of the Air (1869); An Autobiography (1885); and very many
other works. "He has a deep, serious, and almost fanatical reverence
for art."

Assassination of Alexander II., 1881.
Arabi Pasha's Rebellion 1882-83.
War in the Soudan, 1884.

GEORGE ELIOT. 1819-1880. Novelist; poet; essayist.
Scenes of Clerical Life (1858); Adam Bede (1859); and many other
novels down to Daniel Deronda (1876); Spanish Gypsy (1868);
Legend of Jubal (1874).

Murder of Gordon, 1884.
New Reform Bill, 1885.

Echo Library

www.echo-library.com

Echo Library uses advanced digital print-on-demand technology to build and preserve an exciting world class collection of rare and out-of-print books, making them readily available for everyone to enjoy.

Situated just yards from Teddington Lock on the River Thames, Echo Library was founded in 2005 by Tom Cherrington, a specialist dealer in rare and antiquarian books with a passion for literature.

Please visit our website for a complete catalogue of our books, which includes foreign language titles.

The Right to Read

Echo Library actively supports the Royal National Institute of the Blind's Right to Read initiative by publishing a comprehensive range of large print and clear print titles.

Large Print titles are in 16 point Tiresias font as recommended by the RNIB.

Clear Print titles are in 13 point Tiresias font and designed for those who find standard print difficult to read.

Customer Service

If there is a serious error in the text or layout please send details to feedback@echo-library.com and we will supply a corrected copy. If there is a printing fault or the book is damaged please refer to your supplier.

Lightning Source UK Ltd.
Milton Keynes UK
UKOW03f1456240914

239096UK00001B/325/P